insight text guide

Victoria Bladen

Julius Caesar

William Shakespeare

insight®

▸innovative ▸engaging ▸evolving

First published in 2011, reprinted 2012, 2014, 2015, 2020, 2021, 2023, 2024.

Insight Publications Pty Ltd
3/350 Charman Road
Cheltenham VIC 3192
Australia
Tel: +61 3 8571 4950
Email: books@insightpublications.com.au

www.insightpublications.com.au

National Library of Australia Cataloguing-in-Publication entry:

Bladen, Victoria.
William Shakespeare's Julius Caesar / Victoria Bladen.
9781921411885 (pbk.)
For secondary school age.
Shakespeare, William, 1564-1616 Julius Caesar.
Shakespeare, William, 1564-1616—Criticism and interpretation.
822.33

Other ISBNs:
9781922378859 (digital)

Cover design: The Modern Art Production Group

Proudly Printed in Australia by Ligare Book Printers.

contents

CHARACTER MAP

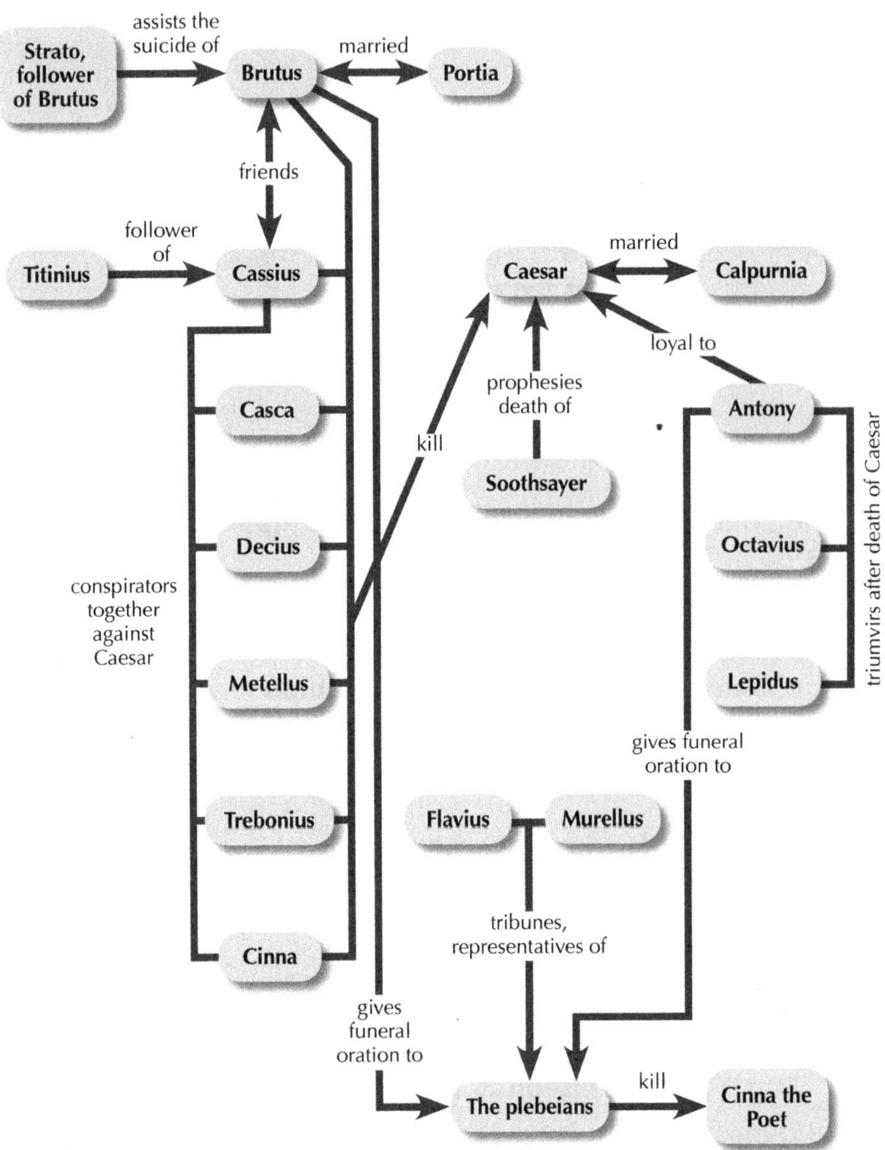

OVERVIEW

William Shakespeare (1564–1616) is one of the most renowned figures of the English literary Renaissance (also referred to as the 'early modern period'). His dramatic and poetic work, written during an intensely productive period from the late sixteenth to the early seventeenth century, has proved capable of enduring well beyond his own time and place. Translated into many languages and adapted for film, television, ballet, opera and graphic novels, Shakespeare's work has evolved into a cultural phenomenon, meaningful and compelling to audiences of different periods and cultures.

Julius Caesar is one of Shakespeare's most well-known plays. This guide is designed to help you navigate your way through the play, organise your thinking and help you write intelligently and competently about the play in your essays and exams. Remember that *Julius Caesar* is a *play*, created to be experienced as a performance onstage, even though it is often first experienced as a written text or as a film. If you are able to see it performed you will gain a deeper understanding of its shape, the characters, how the dramatic action unfolds and the effect of Shakespeare's language. Film adaptations will also help you to understand the play, particularly if you can view different versions. However, remember that watching a film shouldn't be a substitute for a close reading of the text itself.

About the author

So who was Shakespeare? He was born in 1564, when Elizabeth I was on the throne, and died in 1616 when James I was king. Born into a middle-class family in Stratford-upon-Avon (in Warwickshire), William was the son of John Shakespeare, a glove-maker and landowner, and his wife Mary, a gentleman's daughter. He received an education from the King's New School in Stratford, but never attended university. As a young man he fell in love with Anne Hathaway, and they were married in 1582 after Anne became pregnant; the child, Susanna, was born six months after the wedding. Twins, Hamnet and Judith, were born in 1585; Hamnet died when he was a child. Subsequently, the marriage seems to have broken down and when Shakespeare died he left Anne only his 'second-best bed'.

In the late 1580s, Shakespeare moved to London and began his career as a playwright. He joined a theatre company called The Lord Chamberlain's Men (also briefly known as Lord Hunsdon's Men), under the Lord Chamberlain's patronage. The ensemble produced plays that were performed at a venue called the Theatre. He acted in, wrote for and shared in the profits of the theatre company. When the lease over the land on which the Theatre was built expired in 1597, and a dispute with the landlord arose, Shakespeare and his colleagues dismantled the wooden building, took it across the river and reassembled it at Bankside, south of the Thames. The theatre, renamed the Globe, opened in 1599. In London today, a close replica of the Globe stands near the original site, a venue in which Shakespeare's plays are performed all year round.

When James I came to the throne in 1603, he became the patron of the theatre company of which Shakespeare was part owner; the company was therefore renamed the King's Men. The king recognised the huge potential of the theatre to reach many people; in this regard, the theatre can perhaps be thought of as the early seventeenth-century equivalent of television. James wanted his reign to be associated with that 'media' power, despite the fact that in many of Shakespeare's works there is strong criticism of authority figures.

Synopsis

Julius Caesar is a play about political power and how it should be exercised. It raises fundamental questions about the way in which a society should be governed and whether power should be concentrated in one individual or shared between many. The play depicts the final stages of the Roman Republic (a form of government in which the people hold power through their elected representatives and the head of state is appointed or elected). The growing power of Julius Caesar threatens to turn the Republic into a monarchy, wherein supreme authority would be concentrated in one individual, the monarch. Following the death of the monarch, this power and authority would pass to his successor by lineage of blood, not by election or appointment. The play explores the complex question of how the people who are governed should *respond* to the misuse of power. When power is abused, or when subjects disagree with how power is being exercised, what is the right way to act? How should subjects respond to and oppose what they perceive as tyranny? Can an assassination be a just act or is it simply murder? Shakespeare explores the consequences of violence used as a vehicle for political change and the problems that arise from this. As you read *Julius Caesar,* consider what the play suggests about using violence to attempt to achieve a just political state.

The play also explores other significant issues, such as loyalty and friendship. What happens when the duty to act honourably conflicts with loyalties owed to friends or leaders? *Julius Caesar* is also concerned with the power of rhetoric (persuasive speech) and how language can move us to act in certain ways. As a dramatist, Shakespeare was intensely interested in the power of words.

The play begins by presenting a triumphant Caesar in a public space being lauded by a crowd of ordinary Roman workers. Caesar is warned by a soothsayer to be wary of the Ides of March, but he dismisses the man as a dreamer. Brutus and Cassius discuss the growing power of Caesar, and Casca relates to them how Mark Antony publicly offered the crown to Caesar three times. Although Caesar refused the crown, Casca thinks he did so reluctantly. There are concerns that Caesar is a threat to the Republican government of Rome. Cassius flatters Brutus to motivate him to act against Caesar. A strange storm arises and various supernatural events are reported.

In the second act, the night before the Ides of March, Cassius arranges for notes to be sent to Brutus, purportedly from the plebeians, urging him to act against Caesar. Brutus decides that the only way to protect Rome is through the death of Caesar and he, Cassius and others resolve to assassinate Caesar. Portia, Brutus' wife, tries to persuade him to share his heavy secret, but to no avail. Caesar's wife, Calpurnia, experiences dreams and strange events that make her fear for her husband; she tries to persuade him not to go to the Capitol. Caesar is at first persuaded; however, Decius arrives and suggests that Caesar will be seen as a coward if he stays at home. Caesar then resolves to go. Meanwhile Portia is fearful of what is afoot and sends a messenger after Brutus, but after speaking with the Soothsayer, who goes again to warn Caesar, she becomes aware of the assassination plan and appears to support her husband's part in its enactment.

The third act, upon the Ides of March, is the dramatic climax of the play. At the Capitol, Metellus brings a suit to Caesar, which is declined, and at that point the conspirators stab Caesar to death. The conspirators attempt to control public opinion after the deed: Brutus addresses the crowd, arguing that the assassination was necessary, but he then makes the mistake of allowing Mark Antony to speak after him. Antony gives a powerful funeral oration over the body of Caesar with its multiple stab wounds and the crowd is whipped up to a vengeful fury; in their rage, they kill Cinna the Poet.

In the fourth act, Antony, Octavius and Lepidus, as triumvirs, now hold joint power and resolve to move against Brutus, Cassius and the other conspirators. Civil war has broken out in the aftermath of the assassination. However, there is tension within the new alliances; the triumvirs squabble over power sharing, and Brutus and Cassius have a heated argument when Brutus accuses Cassius of taking bribes. They appear to resolve their differences when Brutus reveals the suicide of Portia, yet subsequently they disagree on battle tactics. That night the ghost of Caesar appears to Brutus and foretells his death at Philippi. Brutus realises, to his dismay, that although they killed Caesar, his spirit remains untouched and, if anything, has grown stronger.

In the final act there is tension between Antony and Octavius on the battlefield. The opposing sides trade insults before separating to prepare for battle. Brutus and Cassius say farewell, not knowing whether they will meet again. Cassius commits suicide after misconstruing events on the battlefield, and his follower Titinius does likewise. Brutus, finding Cassius dead, reflects on the continuing power of Caesar. Caesar again appears to him in dreams and Brutus, seeing the end is near, commits suicide by running against the sword he has asked his follower Strato to hold up. Antony and Octavius find Brutus dead, reflect on his nobility and resolve to bury him with full honours.

Character summaries

Brutus

The central character of the play, despite the play's title; intelligent and philosophical, yet naive; close friends with Cassius; strongly loyal to Rome and, paradoxically, to Caesar, despite taking the lead role in the assassination conspiracy.

Cassius

Close friend of Brutus; pragmatic and sly; envious of Caesar; the chief instigator of the conspiracy.

Julius Caesar

Holds the greatest power in Rome; arrogant, egotistical, perceptive of Cassius' envy; sceptical of superstitions and omens; highly conscious of his public persona. The conspirators assassinate Caesar at the Capitol on the Ides of March.

Mark Antony

Deeply loyal to Caesar; wily, intelligent and powerful as a persuasive public speaker; one of the triumvirs after Caesar's death; although hostile to the conspirators, Antony respects and honours Brutus in death.

Portia

Wife of Brutus; strong-willed, well-spoken and courageous; tragically willing to harm herself; ultimately commits suicide.

Calpurnia

Wife of Caesar; a strong speaker; influenced by dreams and omens.

Octavius

One of the triumvirs holding power after the death of Caesar; fights against Brutus and Cassius; argues with Antony over power sharing. The historical figure of Octavius (subsequently renamed Augustus, meaning 'reverend') became the first Roman emperor (from the word 'imperator' meaning 'general'), following the end of the Roman Republic. The play does not cover this subsequent event.

Lepidus

One of the triumvirs holding power after the death of Caesar.

Casca, Trebonius, Decius, Metellus, Ligarius and Cinna

Conspirators who, along with Brutus and Cassius, assassinate Caesar.

Flavius and Murellus

Tribunes, representatives of the plebeians.

The plebeians

The ordinary Roman citizens; not distinguished by separate names in 3.2 and only distinguished by occupation in 1.1. The crowd of common people is an important force in the play.

Soothsayer

Prophesies Caesar's death; warns him to beware the Ides of March; tries again to warn him on the day of the assassination.

Cicero

A senator, representative of the patrician class (upper class) and famous Roman orator and statesman; not involved in the conspiracy.

Cinna the Poet

Killed by the plebeians after Antony's powerful funeral oration when he is mistaken for Cinna the conspirator.

Titinius, Messala and Strato

Followers loyal to Brutus and Cassius.

BACKGROUND & CONTEXT

The play's setting – ancient Rome

According to legend, ancient Rome was founded in the eighth century BC by the brothers Romulus and Remus, sons of Mars (the god of war) and descendants of Aeneas. Their mother Rhea Silvia was imprisoned by Amulius and the children were thrown into the Tiber river; they were washed ashore and suckled by a she-wolf before being found by a herdsman. After killing Remus, Romulus became the first king. Rome developed from a settlement on the Palatine Hill, one of seven hills surrounding the Tiber. The Capitol was the summit of another of the hills and, as the site of a temple dedicated to the god Jupiter, was considered the most sacred part of Rome. Rome was then ruled by a succession of kings, ending with Tarquinius Superbus ('Tarquin the Proud'). The king's son, Sextus, raped Lucretia, the daughter of a celebrated Roman family (Shakespeare's 1594 poem *The Rape of Lucrece* was based on this event). This offence led to the expulsion of the Tarquins from Rome and the establishment of the Roman Republic in 509 BC. Brutus refers to this event in the play: 'Shall Rome stand under one man's awe? What, Rome? / My ancestors did from the streets of Rome / The Tarquin drive when he was called a king' (2.1.52–4).

This system of government gave political rights to at least a certain proportion of the populace, albeit excluding women and non-citizens (slaves and former slaves). Two magistrates (consuls), elected annually from the patrician class (the upper class) replaced the king. At times of national crisis, their powers could be temporarily superseded by the appointment of a dictator. The patricians also elected senators and political decisions were made by the Senate. The plebeians (the lower class) were represented by appointed tribunes and formed their own assembly. After the assassination of Julius Caesar in 44 BC, Octavius (later renamed Augustus) became the first Roman Emperor, thus ending the Republic. From then on, senators appointed the emperor and thus the political system was no longer a form of democracy. *Julius Caesar* is set at the very end of the Republican period, shortly prior to the establishment of the Empire. Thus Shakespeare chose a story situated at a turning point in Rome's history, one with strong dramatic impact.

Shakespeare's historical context

Elizabethan government

In *Julius Caesar*, Brutus and Cassius object to Caesar abusing his position by acting as, and potentially becoming, a monarch. They perceive monarchy as a serious threat to the Roman state. The conspirators assume that absolute power is offensive and dangerous. England's government, at the time Shakespeare was writing the play, was a monarchy, based on the assumption of absolute and divinely ordained power vested in the monarch. Thus we can imagine the fascination that the play, and the political issues it raises, held for Shakespeare's audience at the time. Although the play is about Rome, it was relevant to Shakespeare's England, and remains relevant to contemporary societies in many ways. The stage history of the play includes many interpretations that have transferred the setting to contemporary contexts such as twentieth-century fascism or Latin American dictatorships.

The ideal of Rome

Julius Caesar, like other Shakespeare plays such as *Antony and Cleopatra, Titus Andronicus* and *Coriolanus,* explores ideas about Rome. As a city that was the centre of an extensive empire and then was lost, Rome was a source of intense interest and fascination for Shakespeare and his contemporaries. The English Renaissance, as a literary period, was characterised by a renewed and extensive interest in the works of classical writers from Rome and Greece. Many classical writers, such as Plato (427–347 BC) in his work *The Republic* (c. 375 BC), expressed ideas about how society should be governed, which were of interest to early modern thinkers and writers.

Early modern mythology linked the destiny of Rome to England. The fall of the city of Troy (located in what is now modern-day Turkey) was a well-known story that had been related by the ancient Greek writer Homer and subsequently many others. It told of the 'theft' of the Greek woman Helen, wife of Menelaus, by Paris, a Trojan, and the resulting war between the Greeks and the Trojans. Virgil (70–19 BC), a prominent Roman writer, related in the *Aeneid* (29–19 BC) how Aeneas left the city after the fall of Troy and founded Rome. Early English writers, such as Geoffrey of Monmouth (c. 1100 – c. 54 AD), had chronicled how Lucius Junius Brutus, a descendant of Aeneas, founded the ancient Britons. This founding mythology, which suggested a destiny of national greatness for England, inherited from Rome, added to the English fascination with Roman history. *Julius Caesar* is not simply about the tragic fall of individuals; it also reflects the larger story of Rome, and this is the framework through which Shakespeare's audience approached the story.

Ancient Rome and its people were associated, in the minds of Shakespeare and his contemporaries, with certain characteristics and values. These included honour, constancy (the idea of being stoical and steadfast in the face of adversity), military prowess, virtue, uprightness, order, loyalty, authority and discipline. This differed from how Protestant Elizabethans thought of their contemporary sixteenth-century Italians; they were thought of as untrustworthy, duplicitous and dubious, being Catholics.

The body politic

The concept of the king's two bodies was of central importance to ideas of government in Shakespeare's society. According to this theory the monarch had two bodies: a mortal, physical body that was subject to disease and death, and an immortal, political body that did not die but continued on and was simply transferred to the monarch's successor. Shakespeare plays with this idea in different ways in *Julius Caesar*. The two bodies of Caesar, the physical body and the political body, are inextricably intertwined. Brutus convinces himself that what the conspirators are killing is an abstract, political body, yet in the scene before the crowd, Antony emphasises the vulnerable, physical body of Caesar. Brutus realises, as the play progresses, that in killing Caesar, they have only killed his mortal body and have been unable to kill the idea of Caesar, which, paradoxically, has grown more powerful.

Microcosm and macrocosm

In the early modern period, the human individual was often imagined as a 'little world' (microcosm) reflecting the larger world of the cosmos (macrocosm). It was thought that there were parallels, analogies and correspondences between the two. This idea is drawn on when Brutus observes: 'The genius and the mortal instruments / Are then in council, and the state of a man, / Like to a little kingdom, suffers then / The nature of an insurrection' (2.1.66–9). He imagines his internal conflict over the threat of Caesar's growing power as like a political state suffering an insurrection, thus linking his interior state to that of the larger political state of Rome. Intriguingly, Brutus imagines his inner political state as a monarchy – a 'kingdom' – not a republic.

The crowd

The population of sixteenth-century London was undergoing rapid increases; between 1580 and 1600 the population doubled from approximately 100 000 to 200 000. This created certain problems and issues. Elizabeth I issued certain proclamations in the late sixteenth century in response to what was perceived as overcrowding (although the population was very small in comparison with our contemporary urban populations). One of the effects of the population growth was the potential risk of rebellion. The crowd as a large and potentially unruly mass was something that had to be managed. In the play, Shakespeare presents the Roman crowd as a force that needs to be wooed with words. Brutus, and then Antony, both seek to persuade the crowd to adopt their point of view regarding the assassination. The crowd is presented as a political force whose support is required, an idea that would have been of great interest to Shakespeare's audience, most of whom had no political voice. The threat posed by an unruly crowd is reflected in the horrific scene in 3.3 where the crowd, whipped to a vengeful fury by Antony's speech, kills Cinna the Poet.

Lupercalia

One of the festivals celebrated in ancient Rome was Lupercalia. The event, held in February, honoured Lupercus, the protector of flocks against wolves and a patron of agriculture. As part of the celebrations, youths, 'Luperci', ran around the bounds of the Palatine settlement striking those whom they met, especially women, with strips of goat skin, as a form of fertility magic. The festival also celebrated the founding of Rome by Romulus and Remus, who were suckled by a she-wolf. The festival is significant in the play ('You know it is the feast of Lupercal', 1.1.66) because the play explores events that precipitate a major turning point in Roman history. Like its founding, the shift from a republic to an empire is a pivotal point in the history of Rome.

The four elements and four humours

In the medieval and early modern periods there was a general belief that all sublunary matter (below the level of the moon) was subject to decay and death, and comprised the four elements: earth, fire, air and water. These were also commonly linked with the four humours, which were thought to comprise the body: blood, phlegm, choler and melancholy. The different proportions of these, it was thought, created the personality of a person. This idea is behind Antony's reflection on Brutus: 'His life was gentle, and the elements / So mixed in him that Nature might stand up / And say to all the world, "This was a man!"' (5.5.73–5).

The publication history of *Julius Caesar*

Julius Caesar is generally given a date of composition of 1599, although there is some critical debate on this. There are no surviving draft manuscripts, notes or diaries left by Shakespeare so scholars have to piece together other evidence to determine a date. The earliest recorded performance of the play took place in 1599 and it appeared in print for the first time in the First Folio edition of 1623. This was a compilation of Shakespeare's plays published after his death, organised by a group of his friends to preserve his work.

GENRE, STRUCTURE & LANGUAGE

Genre

A tragedy is a particular form of drama in which death and adversity are central themes. Originating in ancient Greece, tragedy evolved from speeches that accompanied ritual animal sacrifices, and initially comprised only speeches by the Chorus. The innovation of including one actor, and then more, was gradually implemented, with the Chorus 'telling' the story and actors 'showing' the events through dialogue and action.

Tragedy is a genre of excess. In Shakespeare's tragedies there are usually many deaths, with a high body count on the stage by the final scene. This can be a confronting experience. The assassination scene, where Caesar is killed by many stab wounds from the senators, is particularly dramatic, especially when they bathe their hands in his blood after the deed. Tragedy is often a challenge to us because we are used to contemporary stories with 'happy endings'.

Furthermore, the number of deaths generally appears to be greater than seems necessary to punish those with flaws; in other words, the consequences seem out of proportion to the misdeeds. The death of Cinna the Poet, for example, is a point of excess in the play, where the audience feels disturbed and moved by the unnecessary death of an innocent character (also think about the deaths of Portia and Titinius). The excessive number of deaths in a tragedy produces a climax or cathartic experience for the audience. A tragedy usually eliminates many of the principal characters, along with several minor ones, bringing a situation of conflict to a head and clearing the way for future change.

Julius Caesar also has affinities with Shakespeare's history plays in so far as the basic elements of its story are taken from actual historical events. In 44 BC Julius Caesar was assassinated; Shakespeare uses this as the starting point for his play. Shakespeare's primary source was Sir

Thomas North's translation (1579) of the classical writer Plutarch's *Lives of the Noble Grecians and Romanes*. Critics have suggested various other works about Julius Caesar and ancient Rome that may also have inspired Shakespeare. Although he drew from historical sources, the play is nevertheless a particular interpretation of history whereby Shakespeare has imagined the responses of individuals to events and dialogues between characters, and has shaped the historical material in certain ways to achieve particular dramatic effects.

One of the features *Julius Caesar* shares with most tragedies is the sense of impending death, present from the beginning of the play with the warning to Caesar to beware the Ides of March. This anticipation of death is reiterated in premonitions, reports of supernatural events and the language and imagery employed throughout the play. Another aspect of the tragic genre is the idea of flaws in the central characters. Scholars debate whether the play's central tragic character is Caesar or Brutus; both have flaws that lead to their downfall.

Tragedies ultimately present a state of social and political upheaval. There is a cathartic destruction of the current order, from which the only hope, if any, is the possibility that a better world will replace the chaos that has just unfolded. Part of the tragedy of *Julius Caesar* is the ultimate futility of the conspiracy and assassination. Since the play is drawn from well-known historical events, the audience watching the play knows the outcome: the actions of the conspirators do not ensure the survival of the Roman Republic. This dramatic irony, the gap between what the audience knows and the characters don't, adds a sense of futility and doom throughout the play.

Structure

The play is divided into two sections. The first comprises Acts 1 to 3, and relates the events leading up to the assassination of Caesar in 3.1 and its immediate aftermath, concluding with the brutal murder of Cinna the Poet in 3.3. The assassination of Caesar arguably constitutes the dramatic climax of the play, although there are scholarly debates on this since the death of Caesar occurs relatively early and the deaths of Cassius and Brutus provide further points of dramatic intensity in the second section of the play. The second section, comprising Acts 4 and 5, relates the consequences that follow the death of Caesar: the outbreak of civil war. This part of the play presents the conflict between the two factions – one composed of the triumvirs Antony, Octavius and Lepidus (who share the leadership of Rome), and the other composed of Brutus, Cassius and their followers.

There are some notable differences between the two sections of the play. In the first, Shakespeare is concerned with presenting the dangers of excessive power being concentrated in one individual; the arrogance of Caesar and the risk that the Republic will shift to a monarchy create resentment and political unrest, which culminate in the assassination. In the second section, Shakespeare presents the equally difficult problems posed by the vacuum of centralised leadership; tensions arise both in the shared power arrangement of the triumvirate (who argue over power sharing and battle tactics) and between Brutus and Cassius. Another difference is that while the first section is set in Rome's urban spaces, the second section moves beyond urban Rome to the soldiers' camps on the battlefields near Sardis and Philippi. A further difference that marks the division in structure is that in the first section Caesar is a physical entity (although with a strong sense of his abstract, public persona), while in the second he becomes a spirit who appears capable of enacting his revenge on the living.

The structure of the play poses the question: is the tragedy presented by the play Caesar's, Brutus' or Rome's? Although the play is entitled *Julius Caesar*, many critics have argued that the most central and significant figure of the play is Brutus, not Caesar. Brutus was clearly the figure of greatest interest to Shakespeare, since it is he who grapples with the difficult question of how to respond to the growing ambition of Caesar that threatens the ideal of the Roman Republic. Seeing Brutus as the central figure also gives more meaning to the structure of the play, as events continue well after the death of Caesar. Shakespeare was clearly interested in the dramatic potential of difficult decisions and their consequences.

Language

Shakespeare's language can be difficult when encountered for the first time. Some words, which were common at the time, are now unfamiliar, while other words may be familiar but their meanings have changed. The vocabulary definitions throughout the 'Scene-by-scene analysis' will help you interpret the intended meanings. Shakespeare's syntax (the order of words) can also be challenging. Try to gain an overall sense of a passage or scene; this is more important than struggling to understand every sentence. Watching a play or a film will help you, since body language, gesture and tone of voice all add meaning. Also, reading and watching the play more than once will help; with each encounter you will gain new insights and a greater understanding of how Shakespeare's language works.

Shakespeare was a gifted wordsmith, inventing many new words and playing on the multiple meanings or uses of a word (for example, see 1.1.13–17 where the cobbler says 'if you be out, sir, I can mend you' – 'mend' here can be seen as both a reference to mending shoes and an insult). Another aspect of Shakespeare's language that you will notice when studying the play is the constant use of metaphors and similes to describe people, emotions and events. This technique, common in Renaissance literature, adds depth and complexity to the language of the play through the mental images that the words evoke. Cassius says that Caesar 'is now become a god' (1.2.116); although Caesar has not literally become divine, the metaphor expresses how he is perceived and the extent of his excessive power. When Antony uses animal imagery to describe the conspirators he presents them as subject to base, inferior behaviour: 'You showed your teeth like apes and fawned like hounds' (5.1.41). Shakespeare's language is also effective in conveying violence;

note the chilling violence of 'Tear him to pieces' when the plebeians attack Cinna the Poet (3.3.26).

Much of the play is concerned with the power of language and the way in which language can be used to present different viewpoints of the same event. Brutus attempts to construe the killing of Caesar as a sacred ritual duty: 'Let's be sacrificers, but not butchers, Caius. / We all stand up against the spirit of Caesar' (2.1.166–7). He tries to reinforce this idea by directing the assassins to wash their hands in Caesar's blood: 'Stoop, Romans, stoop, / And let us bathe our hands in Caesar's blood / Up to the elbows and besmear our swords' (3.1.105–7). However, Antony portrays the same event in a very different light, using the language of the hunt and figuring the conspirators as hunters with Caesar as their prey:

> Here wast thou bayed, brave hart,
> Here didst thou fall, and here thy hunters stand,
> Signed in thy spoil and crimsoned in thy Lethe.
> O world! Thou wast the forest to this hart,
> And this indeed, O world, the heart of thee.
> How like a deer strucken by many princes
> Dost thou here lie! (3.1.204–10)

Another important aspect of the power of language is the force of rhetoric (persuasive speech). What effect do the funeral orations by Brutus and Antony have on us as the audience? We are drawn, along with the crowd in the play, to agree firstly with Brutus but then we are persuaded by Antony. In this scene there is a strong parallel between the fictional crowd in the play and the live theatre audience: both groups listen to the speakers and are expected to respond to their arguments. By making us aware that both speakers persuade us in different ways, Shakespeare conveys the power of speech and language to move us.

A further aspect of Shakespeare's language that you may notice is the use of lines that seem to 'stand out' from the text. Such lines may be useful as general advice or as a quotation for the audience to remember and use in conversation. Examples include when Caesar says 'Cowards die many times before their deaths, / The valiant never taste of death but once' (2.2.32–3), and when Brutus says 'There is a tide in the affairs of men / Which, taken at the flood, leads on to fortune; / Omitted, all the voyage of their life / Is bound in shallows and in miseries' (4.3.218–21). In Shakespeare's time, short sayings, usually with a didactic function (trying to teach a moral lesson), were popular. Many people going to see Shakespeare's plays would have taken notes of useful 'bite-size' lines they could add to their commonplace books (books that were compilations of useful sayings).

As you are reading the play, note also the rhythm of the language and how this distinguishes speakers. Most of the upper-class characters generally speak in verse, while the lower-class characters usually speak in prose. The verse lines are in iambic pentameter – there are five 'beats' or stresses to the line with unstressed syllables in-between. When this general rule is altered, it is usually to achieve a particular effect. For example Brutus, in his funeral oration, switches to prose, as if trying to emulate the speech of the common Roman. By comparison, Antony speaks in verse, as do the plebeians in sections of this scene. The rhythms of speech can also be effective in conveying violence; note the hostile short sharp lines of the plebeians as they interrogate Cinna the Poet:

> 1 Plebeian: What is your name?
> 2 Plebeian: Whither are you going?
> 3 Plebeian: Where do you dwell? (3.3.5–7)

SCENE-BY-SCENE ANALYSIS

Act 1

1.1 Summary: *The play opens in a public space in Rome. Flavius and Murellus, two tribunes, admonish the common people for coming out to rejoice in Caesar's triumph instead of working.*

The opening scene is set in the streets of Rome where Caesar is returning in triumph after a victory over Pompey. Two tribunes, representatives of the plebeians, are angry with the workers for leaving their work and coming to celebrate and greet Caesar. Flavius and Murellus question some of the workers, a carpenter and a cobbler, and a comic conversation follows. Note that the workers are not given particular names. Referred to only by their occupations, they function as representatives of the ordinary people. Murellus criticises the fickleness of the public, observing that it readily changes allegiance between leaders – a significant point later when the crowd responds to the funeral orations of Brutus and Antony. The celebration also coincides with the feast of Lupercal. Flavius is angry at the people for decorating the statues in celebration of Caesar, and resents Caesar's growing power:

> I'll about
> And drive away the vulgar from the streets;
> So do you too, where you perceive them thick.
> These growing feathers plucked from Caesar's wing
> Will make him fly an ordinary pitch,
> Who else would soar above the view of men
> And keep us all in servile fearfulness. (1.1.68–74)

1.2 Summary: *Caesar is warned by a soothsayer to 'Beware the Ides of March' (1.2.18). Cassius and Brutus discuss the growing power of Caesar. Casca reports to them how Caesar was offered the crown and, although refusing it, seemed to do so reluctantly.*

This scene demonstrates for the audience the extreme power that Caesar wields over those around him. As Antony observes, 'When Caesar says, "Do this", it is performed' (1.2.10). At the same time, such power risks the arousal of resentment and envy in those around him. As Caesar makes his way through the crowd, a soothsayer warns him to be wary of the Ides of March, foreshadowing the assassination. Caesar dismisses the prophecy: 'He is a dreamer' (1.2.24). After Caesar leaves, Brutus and Cassius, two of the senators, have a private conversation. Cassius shows his bitterness towards Caesar, reflecting that although Caesar is treated like a god, he is no different from anyone else: 'I was born free as Caesar, so were you' (1.2.97). Cassius praises Brutus, claiming that Brutus is too humble and unable to see his own greatness: 'And since you know you cannot see yourself / So well as by reflection, I, your glass, / Will modestly discover to yourself / That of yourself which you yet know not of' (1.2.67–70). Cassius' praise is part of his manipulation of Brutus, whom he seeks to motivate to move against Caesar.

Caesar re-enters briefly, speaks to Mark Antony and accurately discerns the ill will Cassius has for him. After he leaves, Casca relates to Brutus and Cassius how Antony offered the crown to Caesar several times and although Caesar refused it, Casca says 'to my thinking he was very loath to lay his fingers off it' (1.2.237–8). The senators are very concerned that the growing power and ambition of Caesar threatens the Republic; if Caesar were to accept the crown, the government would change to a monarchy, vesting complete power in Caesar. After Brutus leaves, Cassius observes to himself how he will attempt to manipulate Brutus into acting with him against Caesar.

1.3 Summary: *A strange storm rages and Casca reports unusual events to Cicero. Cassius reports the conspiracy he is organising; he instructs Cinna to leave forged notes (purporting to be from the people) where Brutus will find them.*

The storm with which the scene opens foreshadows the rising political storm. Casca reports to Cicero the unnatural quality of the storm, paradoxically a 'tempest dropping fire' (1.3.10). The official Elizabethan ideology was that a monarch was God's representative on earth; to harm the bearer of the crown was to go against the natural order of things. Shakespeare's audience would have seen the assassination of Caesar as the equivalent of killing a king (although, ironically, in the play Caesar is killed in an attempt to preserve the Republic from becoming a monarchy) and the unnatural events in nature reflect this upheaval.

While Casca's response to the storm is fear, Cassius has boldly walked the streets, interpreting the 'monstrous quality' (1.3.68) of nature as a warning that the Roman state itself has turned monstrous. Cassius tells Casca that he has orchestrated a group to move against Caesar. He instructs Cinna to leave the forged papers where Brutus will find them, a plan that demonstrates his cunning. The conspirators need the support of Brutus in order to make the assassination appear a worthy act; as Casca observes: 'O, he sits high in all the people's hearts, / And that which would appear offence in us / His countenance, like richest alchemy, / Will change to virtue and to worthiness' (1.3.157–60).

Key point

The first act shows the immense power that Caesar has acquired; workers have left their labour to celebrate his triumph and the senators treat him with excessive deference. Yet Shakespeare also conveys the danger associated with such an exalted position and the resentment it causes. The ominous prophecy of the Soothsayer haunts the first act and the rising storm foreshadows the imminent political crisis.

Vocabulary

Thy (1.1.7): your

Thou (1.1.8): you (subject); suggests familiarity and is generally used for family, friends and to God when praying; can also be used to convey disrespect

Naughty (1.1.15): worthless; worth 'naught'; has stronger connotation of disapproval than in today's usage

Out (1.1.16): at variance; disagreement

Exeunt (1.1.59): stage direction to exit

Capitol (1.1.62): sacred and political centre of Rome

Images (1.1.63): statues

The press (1.2.15): the crowd

Ides of March (1.2.18): the fifteenth of March, according to the old Roman calendar

Strange (1.2.35): unfriendly

Shadow (1.2.58): reflected image

Modestly (1.2.69): without exaggeration

Jealous (1.2.71): mistrustful

Laughter (1.2.72): object of ridicule

Indifferently (1.2.87): equally; without bias

Favour (1.2.91): appearance

Lief (1.2.95): gladly; willingly

Carelessly (1.2.118): unconcernedly

Palm (1.2.131): a branch from a palm tree; a symbol of victory

Colossus (1.2.136): a gigantic statue; the Colossus of Rhodes was one of the Seven Wonders of the Ancient World.

A Brutus (1.2.159): according to Roman legend, Lucius Junius Brutus was the traditional founder of the Roman Republic in the sixth century BC, directing the expulsion of Tarquinius Superbus.

Brooked (1.2.159): endured

Fell (1.2.221): began

Marry (1.2.228): originally an oath, 'by the Virgin Mary', then as a general phrase meaning 'yes, to be sure'

Soft (1.2.245): wait

Falling sickness (1.2.248): epilepsy

Sway (1.3.3): sovereign power

Wonderful (1.3.14): creating awe or astonishment

Drawn (1.3.22): assembled

Prodigies (1.3.28): something extraordinary

Unbracèd (1.3.48): unprotected; unclothed

Fleering (1.3.117): laughing coarsely

Pompey's Porch (1.3.126): space adjoining a theatre built by Pompey; historically the place where the assassination of Caesar takes place. Shakespeare changed this location to the Capitol.

Praetor (1.3.143): position just below a consul; a civil and military magistrate

Alchemy (1.3.159): the (mythical) process of turning base metal into gold. In Shakespeare's time many people believed this was possible and alchemists claimed to be able to do this.

Q In 1.2, Cassius is resentful of the fact that Caesar is a mortal man yet is treated like a god. Why was this issue of central importance to Shakespeare's Elizabethan audience?

Q In 1.3, Cicero observes, 'men may construe things after their fashion / Clean from the purpose of the things themselves' (1.3.34–5). Describe two different ways that the storm is interpreted in 1.3 and by whom.

Act 2

2.1 Summary: *Brutus, in his orchard, debates with himself how to respond to the threat of Caesar's power. He reads a note that appears to be from the people (but which Cassius has written). The conspirators arrive at his house and successfully persuade him to join the rebellion. After they leave, Portia attempts to persuade Brutus to let her into his confidence.*

Brutus, in his orchard on the night before the Ides of March, contemplates what must be done in relation to Caesar. Unlike Cassius, Brutus does not bear personal enmity towards Caesar: 'And for my part / I know no personal cause to spurn at him / But for the general. He would be crowned' (2.1.10–12). As he grapples mentally with the threat that Caesar poses, Lucius brings him a note to which Brutus responds: 'Thus must I piece it out: / Shall Rome stand under one man's awe? What, Rome?' (2.1.51–2). Brutus believes this note is from the people of Rome urging him to act and it is to this idea, of the people of Rome as a single entity, that he responds: 'O Rome, I make thee promise, / If the redress will follow, thou receivest / Thy full petition at the hand of Brutus' (2.1.56–8).

Cassius and the other conspirators arrive. Note how Brutus describes the conspiracy as an abstract idea with a 'monstrous visage' (2.1.81); although he feels that killing Caesar is the right thing to do ('It must be by his death', 2.1.10), he is not blind to the horror of the action. Cassius again stresses the high regard that the Romans have for Brutus, who is now clearly resolved to act with the conspirators. Cassius proposes that they all swear an oath but Brutus disagrees, arguing that their cause is so righteous it should be sufficient motivation in itself and that an oath would 'stain / The even virtue of our enterprise' (2.1.132–3). Brutus seeks to frame the assassination as a noble and justifiable deed. Cassius proposes that they also kill Mark Antony, since he is loyal to Caesar, but Brutus disagrees: 'our course will seem too bloody' (2.1.162). Brutus is concerned about how the action will look to the public, and there is no political justification for killing Antony. Cassius is pragmatic; Brutus is an idealist.

When the conspirators leave, we see an encounter between Brutus and Portia, his wife, which emphasises the impact of his public actions on his domestic life. Portia is deeply concerned about the changes in Brutus' behaviour, and accurately gauges that something significant is going on: 'You have some sick offence within your mind, / Which by the right and virtue of my place / I ought to know of' (2.1.268–70). She implores Brutus to take her into his confidence. Note that in the male-dominated Roman world that gives little status to women, Portia feels forced to act like a man in order to be respected: 'I have made strong proof of my constancy, / Giving myself a voluntary wound / Here, in the thigh. Can I bear that with patience / And not my husband's secrets?' (2.1.299–302). Portia wounds herself because she believes that bearing physical pain is the only way she will be respected by her husband sufficiently to be treated as an equal in the public, political sphere. Although Brutus promises to tell her his secret, he is sidetracked by the arrival of Ligarius and exits with him.

2.2 Summary: *Calpurnia, who has had ominous dreams, pleads with Caesar to stay home. At first she manages to persuade him, but Decius arrives and changes Caesar's mind.*

Calpurnia is stricken with fear and foreboding for Caesar as a result of her dreams and the various unnatural events occurring in the Capitol; however, Caesar raises various arguments in objection to her request that he stay at home. He argues that no one can avoid the fate ordained by the gods ('What can be avoided / Whose end is purposed by the mighty gods?', 2.2.26–7) and that the prophetic signs are just as likely to be for others as for him (2.2.28–9). To this argument Calpurnia retorts that nature only responds to events affecting princes, not beggars (2.2.30–1). (Her reference to 'princes' ironically signals why Caesar is in danger – for being thought of as a potential monarch.) Caesar also asserts his courage: 'Cowards die many times before their deaths, / The valiant never taste of death but once' (2.2.32–3). Even so, he requests his priests to carry out a sacrifice. Just as the storm was interpreted differently in 1.3, when Caesar's augurers cannot find the heart of the sacrificed animal and interpret this as a warning, Caesar interprets it as a sign not to be a coward (2.2.41–3).

Note that Caesar constantly refers to himself in the third person: 'Caesar shall go forth' (2.2.48). This emphasises the distinction between Caesar as an ordinary man and the idea of Caesar as a public entity. Although at first Caesar agrees to Calpurnia's request not to go to the Capitol (2.2.55–6), Decius is able to change Caesar's mind by cunningly suggesting that if he stays away he will be thought a coward. Caesar thus resolves to go forth: 'How foolish do your fears seem now, Calpurnia! /

I am ashamèd I did yield to them' (2.2.105–6). Note again that Shakespeare is interested in the power of rhetoric to persuade a person to act first in one way and then in another. Brutus, Antony and the other senators then arrive to escort Caesar.

2.3 Summary: *Artemidorus reads a warning note he intends to give to Caesar. Although Artemidorus is a separate character to the Soothsayer, in performance the same actor usually plays both these roles.*

2.4 Summary: *Portia, frantic with concern for Brutus, sends Lucius to the Senate House and then encounters the Soothsayer.*

The Soothsayer enters and tells Portia that he will appeal to Caesar 'to befriend himself' (2.4.30), seeking to warn him again. Portia's change of attitude here is ambiguous and is the subject of debate by critics. She appears to realise that Brutus intends to harm Caesar and to support him in this. Seeing her husband as bold and courageous for his intended political action, she chastises herself: 'how weak a thing / The heart of woman is!' (2.4.39–40). This expresses the common Elizabethan prejudice against women that saw them as weaker and less virtuous than men.

Key point

Shakespeare makes the issue of how to respond to the threat of Caesar complex because, as Caesar has not actually accepted the crown, the conspirators are only acting on an assumption that he will become a monarch and a tyrant: 'he may do danger' (2.1.17); 'So Caesar may. / Then lest he may, prevent' (2.1.27–8). This complexity, how to respond to an anticipated threat, affects the question of whether the assassination can be viewed as an honourable and justifiable action.

Vocabulary

Exhalations (2.1.44): meteors

Genius (2.1.66): according to pagan belief, this was a spirit given to every person at birth that would determine their character and fortune.

Brother (2.1.70): Cassius is Brutus' brother-in-law; he married Brutus' sister

Path (2.1.83): pursue one's course

Palter (2.1.126): shift position

Take thought (2.1.187): become melancholy

Augurers (2.1.200): priests who foretell the future

Figures (2.1.231): imaginary forms

Humours (2.1.262): moisture; vapours

Gods (2.2.27): these are the classical pagan gods, led by Jupiter, the father of the gods. Although Shakespeare's society was predominantly Christian, *Julius Caesar* was set before Christianity.

Earns (2.2.129): grieves

Beseech (2.4.30): plead; persuade

Suit (2.4.42): request for a favour

Q Analyse the thoughts of Brutus in his orchard in 2.1. What are his reasons for moving against Caesar?

Q What are the reasons Caesar gives for wanting to go forth to the Capitol in 2.2?

Act 3

3.1 Summary: *The climax of the play; Caesar is assassinated at the Capitol. The conspirators then reflect on what they have done. Mark Antony reacts in grief and anger, but prudently appears to support the conspirators and asks that he be allowed to give a public funeral oration.*

The Soothsayer and Artemidorus attempt to give their final warnings to Caesar, but he ignores them and proceeds to the Capitol. Metellus Cimber puts a suit forward for the repeal of his brother's banishment, which Caesar refuses, asserting his constancy in making decisions. 'I am constant as the northern star, / Of whose true-fixed and resting quality / There is no fellow in the firmament' (3.1.60–2). Yet this simile has the effect of emphasising Caesar's arrogance, as does his next metaphor in 'Wilt thou lift up, Olympus?' (3.1.74) which equates him with the home of the gods.

The conspirators then attack him with knives. Caesar's famous line: '*Et tu, Brute?* – Then fall, Caesar!' (3.1.77) expresses Caesar's shock that one of his most trusted senators is part of the conspiracy; that is, if Brutus is against him, then there is no hope. Note the importance of language after the death of Caesar. Cinna claims 'Liberty! Freedom! Tyranny is dead!' (3.1.78), identifying Caesar as the personification of tyranny. Brutus paradoxically claims that the conspirators are 'Caesar's friends' (3.1.104), based on the idea that they were opposed to the political persona of Caesar, not to the person himself.

Brutus urges them to wash their hands in Caesar's blood as if the act was noble and sacred. However, as several critics have observed, it is likely that Shakespeare was alluding to the practice of hunters dipping their hands in the blood of slain animals – an allusion which suggests that the act was a murderous hunt, not a sacred duty.

When Antony arrives, the audience is given a different perspective on the assassination. He mourns Caesar and expresses wonder that such a person, who was depicted publicly as superhuman, was nevertheless mortal: 'O mighty Caesar! Dost thou lie so low? / Are all thy conquests, glories, triumphs, spoils / Shrunk to this little measure?' (3.1.148–50). He refers to the conspirators as 'hunters' (3.1.205). Brutus attempts to justify their actions, separating their hands, which committed the murder, from their hearts, which he describes as 'pitiful' (meaning 'full of pity', 3.1.169). When Antony asks to give a funeral oration to the crowd in the presence of Caesar's body, Brutus agrees. Cassius, however, is more perceptive than Brutus and realises Antony's power to move the crowd: 'Know you how much the people may be moved / By that which he will utter' (3.1.234–5). Antony prophesies over the body of Caesar that his death will result in civil war: 'Cry havoc and let slip the dogs of war' (3.1.273).

3.2 Summary: *Brutus and then Antony address the crowd of plebeians. At first they are swayed by Brutus; however, they are soon persuaded to accept Antony's point of view, particularly in the powerful presence of Caesar's corpse. Whipped into a frenzy, the crowd leaves, promising revenge on the conspirators.*

This scene is a powerful one and productions of the play often place the plebeians among the theatre audience, which emphasises the connection between the fictional crowd and the live audience; both are called upon to judge what has occurred. Brutus and Antony represent two sides of the debate, each of which has strong arguments. Brutus speaks in prose, the language form of the ordinary people, rather than in verse, which Shakespeare usually gives to upper-class characters (although, paradoxically Shakespeare has the plebeians speaking in verse, which conveys the political voice and power the ordinary people are attributed with in this scene). Brutus claims that he loved Caesar: 'If then that friend demand why Brutus rose against Caesar, this is my answer: not that I loved Caesar less, but that I loved Rome more' (3.2.18–20). Thus Brutus argues that he acted in the best interests of Rome and was protecting the Republic. The plebeians agree: 'This Caesar was a tyrant. / Nay, that's certain: / We are blest that Rome is rid of him' (3.2.61–2). Ironically, one of the plebeians says of Brutus: 'Let him be Caesar' (3.2.43) which suggests that at least some of the crowd want a replacement all-powerful leader rather than the opportunity to establish a true democracy.

Antony understands the power of bringing the body of Caesar out into the public space. The abstract ideals of Brutus pale in comparison with the devastating impact of physical reality and the dramatic effect of showing the crowd precisely where the daggers penetrated the mantle of Caesar. The crowd quickly changes its mind about the conspirators: 'They were traitors' (3.2.145); 'Slay! Let not a traitor live!' (3.2.196). Antony also makes effective use of Caesar's will, telling the crowd that Caesar has bequeathed them money and public space (3.2.231–41), thus portraying Caesar as a democratic and caring leader. Once the crowd exits in a murderous fury, Antony reveals his full knowledge of the effect of his speech: 'Now let it work. Mischief, thou art afoot, / Take thou what course thou wilt!' (3.2.250–1).

3.3 Summary: *The crowd, in a frenzy, kills Cinna the Poet.*

The crowd is brutal and bullying in its brief interrogation of Cinna the Poet, which quickly results in the decision to kill him: 'Tear him to pieces, he's a conspirator' (3.3.26). Shakespeare presents the crowd as unable to act rationally; the world of Rome that Brutus sought to preserve has instead descended into murderous chaos.

Key point

After the assassination, the conspirators reflect on how they will be viewed by history and imagine the scene being replayed in the theatre (which is precisely what happens every time the play is performed): 'How many ages hence / Shall this our lofty scene be acted over / In states unborn and accents yet unknown!' (3.1.111–13). Such moments in a play, which reflect on play-acting itself, are known as metadramatic. In one sense the historical events depicted can't be separated from the plays and books that tell stories of them.

Vocabulary

Hail (3.1.3): greeting

Doth (3.1.4): does

Touches (3.1.7): affects; concerns

Sirrah (3.1.10): used when referring to someone of a lower social status; usually an insult

Mark (3.1.18): take notice; observe

Puissant (3.1.33): powerful

Couchings (3.1.36): subservient bowing

Courtesies (3.1.36): curtsies

Preordinance and first decree (3.1.38): traditional laws and customs

Fond (3.1.39): foolish; credulous

Spaniel fawning (3.1.43): loving attention like that from a dog; flattery; intended as an insult

Cur (3.1.46): dog; vicious or cowardly person

Enfranchisement (3.1.57): restored as a citizen of Rome

Firmament (3.1.62): heavens

Sparks (3.1.63): stars

Apprehensive (3.1.67): comprehending; able to understand

Speak hands (3.1.76): this refers to the hands of the conspirators; a call to action

Et tu, Brute? (3.1.77): Latin; translates as 'you too, Brutus?'

Abide (3.1.94): suffer the consequences of; be tied to

Abridged (3.1.104): shortened

Lofty (3.1.112): exalted

Knot (3.1.117): group

Soft (3.1.122): wait

Vouchsafe (3.1.130): confirm; guarantee

Misgiving (3.1.145): worry; fear

Reek and smoke (3.1.158): covered with fresh blood

Brothers' temper (3.1.175): temperament of a brother (i.e. mildness and friendliness towards Antony)

Multitude (3.1.180): crowd of ordinary people

Bayed (3.1.204): controlled and cornered; like prey being barked at by dogs

Lethe (3.1.206): the river of forgetfulness in Hades, the underworld

Wast (3.1.207): was

Dost (3.1.210): do

Pricked (3.1.216): marked

Pulpit (3.1.229): raised platform from which to speak

Ate (3.1.271): personifies moral blindness; daughter of Strife and sister of Lawlessness; a figure of revenge

Carrion (3.1.275): dead; corpse

Corse (3.1.291); corpse

Rude (3.2.26): lowly; base

Interred (3.2.68): buried

Coffers (3.2.81): money chests

Methinks (3.2.100): I think

Drachmaes (3.2.232): silver coins

Whither (3.3.6): where

Q Why do you think Shakespeare includes the harrowing scene of the crowd murdering Cinna the Poet?

Q Analyse the arguments of Brutus and Antony in 3.2. How does each speaker seek to persuade the plebeians to his point of view?

Act 4

4.1 Summary: *Antony, Octavius and Lepidus agree to divide the Roman world between them, and discuss revenge against the conspirators.*

The fourth act depicts the aftermath of the death of Caesar. Power in the Roman world is now to be shared three ways between Mark Antony, Octavius and Lepidus, the triumvirs. However, there are problems with the agreement right from the start. After Lepidus exits, Antony slanders him: 'This is a slight, unmeritable man' (4.1.12). There is also tension between Antony and Octavius, each seeing himself as superior, with Antony claiming: 'Octavius, I have seen more days than you' (4.1.18). While the three propose to form an alliance to fight against Brutus and Cassius, this ill-feeling does not augur well for a strong united front.

4.2 Summary: *The relationship between Brutus and Cassius is also under strain and they begin to argue.*

The strong friendship between Brutus and Cassius has soured and Brutus observes: 'When love begins to sicken and decay / It useth an enforcèd ceremony' (4.2.20–1). Cassius arrives and accuses Brutus of wronging him, while Brutus urges Cassius to be discreet about their differences. Brutus perceives the importance of appearing to have a united front: 'Before the eyes of both our armies here – / Which should perceive nothing but love from us – / Let us not wrangle' (4.3.43–5).

4.3 Summary: *Brutus accuses Cassius of taking bribes and a heated argument follows, although they eventually manage to resolve their differences. Brutus discloses that Portia has committed suicide. That night the ghost of Caesar appears to Brutus.*

In the heated argument between Brutus and Cassius, both characters present their version of events. Brutus is incensed that Cassius would act in a corrupt manner; he needs to maintain his belief in their integrity and virtue in order to feel that they acted justly against Caesar: 'Did not great Julius bleed for justice' sake?' (4.3.19); 'shall we now / Contaminate our fingers with base bribes' (4.3.23–4). However, Cassius sees Brutus as betraying their friendship, arguing that 'A friend should bear his friend's infirmities' (4.3.86).

After they make up, Brutus reveals that Portia has committed suicide. Elizabethans perceived Romans as being particularly stoic; that is, able to bear suffering with fortitude. Brutus embodies this notion; he does not show excessive emotion in discussing her death and is philosophical about it, as when he tells his friend 'We must die, Messala / With meditating that she must die once, / I have the patience to endure it now' (4.3.190–2). The conversation shifts to battle tactics and Brutus and Cassius disagree about a decision to march to Philippi, which again points to the tension in their friendship.

At night Caesar's ghost appears to Brutus. When Brutus asks what he is, the ghost replies: 'Thy evil spirit, Brutus' (4.3.282), which suggests that the ghost in some way is the dark side (or the guilty conscience) of Brutus. The ghost prophesies that Brutus will see him at Philippi, foreshadowing Brutus' death.

Key point

Just as Shakespeare, in the first three acts, presented the problems arising from the concentration of too much power in one individual, in the last two acts, he depicts the chaos arising from a lack of central leadership and unstable political relationships.

Vocabulary

Threefold world (4.1.14): refers to the traditional division of the known world into three parts: Europe, Asia and Africa. After the discovery of America in the late fifteenth century, a fourth continent was added to this conception.

Commons (4.1.27): common land that belongs to everyone in the community

Provender (4.1.30): fodder for livestock

Salutation (4.2.5): greeting

Mettle (4.2.24): strength

Jades (4.2.26): overworked horses

Quartered (4.2.28): accommodated

Itching palm (4.3.10): taking bribes; corruption

Slight (4.3.37): insignificant; inferior

Choler (4.3.39); *choleric* (4.3.43): anger; angry

Fret (4.3.42): worry

Spleen (4.3.47): internal organ thought to be responsible for passion and sudden emotion

Legions (4.3.76): large units of soldiers. Legions were divided into cohorts, which were themselves divided into centuries of one hundred soldiers. Ordinary soldiers were called legionaries.

Rascal (4.3.80): wretched; base

Counters (4.3.80): counterfeit coins; spoken of contemptuously

Rived (4.3.85); torn; split

Olympus (4.3.92): the mountain where the gods live

Pluto (4.3.102): refers to Plutus, a figure from Greek myth who personified wealth; often confused with Pluto, god of the underworld, since he too was associated with wealth coming from the earth

Sheathe (4.3.107): put away into its cover

Yokèd (4.3.110): tied to

Rash humour (4.3.120): choler, one of the four humours

Meet (4.3.125): appropriate

Saucy (4.3.134): impertinent

Distract (4.3.155): became anxious

Pledge (4.3.160): promise

Taper (4.3.164): candle

Order of proscription (4.3.180): declaration that a Roman citizen is now an outlaw and their goods are to be confiscated

'Twixt (4.3.204): between

Ripe (4.3.215): ready for action; at the peak

Ventures (4.3.224): investment in a ship's cargo. An adventurer was a person who risked his venture.

Knave (4.3.241): person of inferior status; can be used as an insult

Mace (4.3.268): staff used by a bailiff to touch a person being arrested

Bid (4.3.307): ask; direct

Q Analyse the argument between Brutus and Cassius in 4.3. What do their arguments reveal about their characters and values?

Q What is the dramatic effect of the appearance of Caesar's ghost? Compare this with other references to the supernatural that occur throughout the play.

Act 5

5.1 Summary: *Tension continues between Octavius and Antony. The opposing sides of the civil war confront each other. Before leaving for battle, Brutus and Cassius say their final farewell.*

Octavius and Antony bicker as they join their army. Antony tells Octavius to take the left side of the field. Octavius disagrees with this tactic and tells Antony to take the left side himself, to which Antony responds 'Why do you cross me in this exigent?' (5.1.19). Again, Shakespeare points to the difficulties of a shared leadership. The opponents in the civil war face each other and trade insults. Antony suggests that the conspirators were no more than deceptive and savage animals: 'You showed your teeth like apes and fawned like hounds' (5.1.41) and Octavius calls them 'traitors' (5.1.55). Brutus refuses to see himself in this way: 'thou canst not die by traitors' hands / Unless thou bring'st them with thee' (5.1.56–7).

The two sides separate and Brutus and Cassius say farewell in a moving scene. Brutus says 'whether we shall meet again I know not, / Therefore our everlasting farewell take: / For ever and for ever, farewell, Cassius!' (5.1.114–16).

5.2 Summary: *Brutus dispatches Messala with orders for the soldiers.*

5.3 Summary: *Cassius misinterprets events in the chaos of the battlefield and, in despair, commits suicide.*

Cassius kills his flag bearer for retreating in fear; he resents such cowardly behaviour which fails to uphold the high standards of bravery expected of Romans (5.3.3–4). Cassius sends Titinius to find out what is happening, and then sends Pindarus to observe Titinius. Pindarus mistakenly reports that Titinius is surrounded by the enemy so Cassius, in despair, asks Pindarus to kill him: 'Caesar, thou art revenged / Even with the sword that killed thee' (5.3.45–6). Titinius and Messala enter and Messala reports the current state of the battle: Brutus has the upper hand over Octavius; however, Antony has overpowered the legions of Cassius. Titinius, discovering the death of Cassius, laments that Cassius 'hast misconstrued everything' (5.3.84) and then also commits suicide. Committing suicide, which was a sin according to Christian ideology, was regarded by Elizabethans as a particularly Roman act; this is reflected in Titinius saying 'This is a Roman's part' (5.3.89).

Brutus, reflecting upon the death of his friend, observes 'O Julius Caesar, thou art mighty yet, / Thy spirit walks abroad and turns our swords / In our own proper entrails' (5.3.94–6). There is a strong sense of Caesar's revenge being enacted in this last act.

5.4 Summary: *Lucilius impersonates Brutus to protect him, and is captured by Antony's faction.*

Lucilius observes that 'no enemy / Shall ever take alive the noble Brutus. / The gods defend him from so great a shame!' (5.4.21–3). This reflects the heroic, masculine code that Brutus and the other Roman soldiers observe, pursuant to which death is preferable to (and more noble than) being taken prisoner by the enemy.

5.5 Summary: *Brutus, feeling that his hour is up, asks each of his companions to kill him. Strato assists him to commit suicide. In the final scene of the play, Antony, Octavius and others enter and reflect on the nobility of Brutus.*

Brutus observes that the ghost of Caesar has visited him again and thus that the end is near: 'I know my hour is come' (5.5.20). He sees greater honour in committing suicide than being killed by the enemy: 'Our enemies have beat us to the pit. / It is more worthy to leap in ourselves / Than tarry till they push us' (5.5.23–5). However, his companions are reluctant to help Brutus commit suicide; as Volumnius observes, 'That's not an office for a friend, my lord' (5.5.29). Strato agrees to help and holds Brutus' sword for him to run onto. Brutus perceives the act as completing the revenge of Caesar: 'Caesar, now be still, / I killed not thee with half so good a will' (5.5.50–1).

Antony, Octavius, Messala and Lucilius enter, and Strato reports the death of Brutus. In this final scene of the play it is significant that Antony reflects on the virtue of Brutus: 'This was the noblest Roman of them all: / All the conspirators, save only he, / Did that they did in envy of great Caesar. / He only, in a general honest thought / And common good to all, made one of them' (5.5.68–72). Thus Brutus is seen as a person who acted honourably, in comparison with the other conspirators who, Antony asserts, acted for selfish reasons.

Key point

Both Cassius and Brutus perceive their deaths as a form of revenge by Caesar; the effect is of Caesar continuing to be a strong spiritual presence after his death.

Vocabulary

Exigent (5.1.19): a critical, urgent moment

Hybla bees (5.1.34): Hybla is a town in Sicily famous for its honey

Bills (5.2.1): written orders

Ensign (5.3.3): flag bearer

Spur (5.3.29): a ridge projecting from the side of a mountain or hill

Spurs (5.3.30): sharp spikes for hurting a horse (to make it go faster)

Hither (5.3.36): here

Hilts (5.3.43): handle

Durst (5.3.48): if; should

Room ho (5.4.16): make room

Prithee (5.5.44): pray you; please

Smatch (5.5.46): taste

Q What do the suicides in Act 5 reveal about Roman values?

Q Why do Antony and Octavius declare their respect for Brutus in the final scene of the play?

CHARACTERS & RELATIONSHIPS

In the medieval theatre that predated Shakespeare, characters had less depth and were generally embodiments of abstract ideas such as vice, or figures known to the audience from biblical stories or historical tales. They fulfilled prescribed roles and functions in a play, making it less important to provide details of the characters since they were subservient to the overall structure of the play. Shakespeare is often credited with being among the first playwrights to provide a greater interiority to his characters. By that, critics mean that he gives us more information about what the characters think and how they feel than playwrights had previously provided. We can, therefore, construct a psychological profile for the characters. This depth is not provided uniformly across the characters; we learn more about some characters than others. There is also often a complexity to Shakespeare's characters that makes us respond to them as plausible people rather than types (characters that represent certain ideas or embody particular characteristics). Virtually none of Shakespeare's characters can be reduced to simple stereotypes; there are often flaws in his heroes and elements of virtue in his villains.

Brutus

Key quotes

... I love
The name of honour more than I fear death. (1.2.88–9)

Let's be sacrificers, but not butchers, Caius.
We all stand up against the spirit of Caesar,
And in the spirit of men there is no blood.
O, that we then could come by Caesar's spirit
And not dismember Caesar! But, alas,
Caesar must bleed for it. And, gentle friends,
Let's kill him boldly, but not wrathfully;
Let's carve him as a dish fit for the gods,
Not hew him as a carcass fit for hounds. (2.1.166–74)

Brutus is presented as a thoughtful, intelligent and introspective thinker. He weighs the issue of the threat Caesar presents to the Republic carefully in his mind before acting. The decision is made more difficult because Caesar is his friend, and one who thinks highly of him. Brutus must decide between the public good of Rome, as he sees it, and his personal friendship with and respect for Caesar. We see both the private and public sides of Brutus through his relationship with his wife Portia. Although she implores him to take her into his confidence, Brutus separates his public action from the private domestic sphere, in which he perceives his wife belongs, and doesn't tell her what's on his mind.

Brutus is perceived as an honourable and virtuous character in the play, yet he also makes some significant errors of judgment. What might we classify as Brutus' flaws? Some critics have pointed to his failure to perceive things as they really are. His political idealism arguably undermines his ostensible nobility and virtue. Brutus believes, and claims, that he is acting in the best interests of the state, so how is this idea undermined? The fact that the audience sees the machinations of Cassius in prompting Brutus to act (an example of dramatic irony) undermines the validity of the venture from the start – we can see that Brutus is acting partly as a result of Cassius' manipulation of him. A forged letter appeals to Brutus' ego and urges him to be a man of action: 'Brutus, thou sleep'st. Awake, and see thyself! / Shall Rome, etc. Speak, strike, redress!' (2.1.46–7).

Brutus, attempting to frame the assassination as a sacred act, refers to the 'virtue of our enterprise' (2.1.133) and sees the conspirators as acting for the good of the people and for Rome as a whole. This is the only basis on which Brutus would act: 'What is it that you would impart to me? / If it be aught toward the general good, / Set honour in one eye and death I'th'other / And I will look on both indifferently' (1.2.84–7). Yet other language Shakespeare uses to describe the assassination, such as that used by Antony (3.1.204–10) and Cassius ('the work we have in hand, / Most bloody, fiery, and most terrible', 1.3.129–30), counteracts and undermines this idealised analysis by Brutus. The effect of this is to set up a division between the perspective of Brutus and that of others, which suggests a degree of self-delusion in Brutus. The high standing of Brutus and his reputation for honour are needed by the other conspirators to render the enterprise virtuous. As Casca observes, 'O, he sits high in all the people's hearts, / And that which would appear offence in us / His countenance, like richest alchemy, / Will change to virtue and to worthiness' (1.3.157–60). The effect is to make truth mutable; whether the action is honourable or not thus appears open to interpretation.

The idealism of Brutus also puts the conspirators at risk; his sense of honour will not allow him to kill Antony along with Caesar, contrary to the pragmatic and accurate (albeit brutal) view of Cassius that it would be dangerous to let Antony live (2.1.156–61). Similarly, Cassius is more pragmatic on the battlefield but Brutus overrules him (4.3.203). It is through the character of Brutus that Shakespeare explores the gap between human idealism and reality.

Key point

Brutus seeks to portray the assassination of Caesar in exalted terms, as a sacred act in defence of the Republic, rather than a base act of simple murder. How does Shakespeare expose the problems with this viewpoint? In the funeral oration of Antony, we perceive a key conflict: Brutus is seen as an honourable man, a person who acts for the good of others, so how can this be reconciled with a person who has committed murder?

Cassius

Key quotes

A friend should bear his friend's infirmities. (4.3.86)

I that denied thee gold will give my heart:
Strike as thou didst at Caesar. For I know
When thou didst hate him worst thou loved'st him better
Than ever thou loved'st Cassius. (4.3.104–7)

Cassius is presented from the start of the play as duplicitous and untrustworthy. He accurately discerns the essentially good nature of

Brutus and knows that he will need to manipulate Brutus in order to persuade him to act against Caesar: 'Well, Brutus, thou art noble; yet I see / Thy honourable metal may be wrought / From that it is disposed' (1.2.297–9). The metaphor of Brutus as metal, which may be worked, emphasises how Cassius needs to manipulate Brutus to rebel against Caesar. Although Brutus is a close friend of Cassius, he is unable to discern Cassius' deceptive nature. Perhaps Brutus does perceive some menace in Cassius, yet he allows the appeal to his ego to override such doubts: 'Into what dangers would you lead me, Cassius, / That you would have me seek into myself / For that which is not in me?' (1.2.63–5). By comparison, Caesar accurately perceives the danger Cassius poses for him, using the metaphor of hunger to convey the envy and ambition of Cassius: 'Let me have men about me that are fat, / Sleek-headed men and such as sleep a-nights. / Yond Cassius has a lean and hungry look, / He thinks too much: such men are dangerous' (1.2.192–5).

While Brutus acts out of loyalty towards Rome, a significant motivation for Cassius is envy and resentment: 'And this man / Is now become a god, and Cassius is / A wretched creature and must bend his body / If Caesar carelessly but nod on him' (1.2.115–18). At the same time, the views of Cassius are an accurate and perceptive political critique. There is no physical difference between Caesar and any other human; Caesar too can be subject to physical illness (1.2.119) and be at risk in a river torrent (1.2.100–15). It is interesting to note that in telling his story of rescuing Caesar, Cassius likens himself to the legendary Aeneas who bore his father on his back when leaving burning Troy, according to Virgil's *Aeneid*. By comparing himself to a heroic figure associated with Rome's founding, Cassius shows himself to be susceptible to hubris, the quality he resents in Caesar.

Another important aspect of Cassius is his loyalty to Brutus. Though he manipulates him, there is no question that he has a strong love for Brutus and is deeply offended when Brutus accuses him of corruption. Cassius places more weight on friendship than on the ethics of taking bribes: 'Brutus hath rived my heart. / A friend should bear his friend's infirmities, / But Brutus makes mine greater than they are' (4.3.85–7). He expects his friend to overlook what he sees as minor faults. Brutus, by comparison, is mortified that Cassius would 'Contaminate our fingers with base bribes / And sell the mighty space of our large honours / For so much trash as may be graspèd thus?' (4.3.24–6).

Key point

Caesar's elevation to a position of extreme power is a human construction rather than a natural state of affairs: 'I was born free as Caesar, so were you' (1.2.97). Cassius questions the right of Caesar to this position – 'Why should that name be sounded more than yours?' (1.2.143) – and so provides an important dissenting voice in the play, one that would have been of great interest to Shakespeare's audience who, as subjects with negligible power, were told that their monarch was divinely appointed.

Caesar

Key quotes

Why, man, he doth bestride the narrow world
Like a Colossus, and we petty men
Walk under his huge legs and peep about
To find ourselves dishonourable graves. (Cassius, 1.2.135–8)

O mighty Caesar! Dost thou lie so low?
Are all thy conquests, glories, triumphs, spoils
Shrunk to this little measure? (Antony, 3.1.148–50)

Throughout the play we are presented with different ideas about Caesar, sometimes through his own words, but more often through the voices of other characters. The excessive reverence shown to Caesar is constantly emphasised in the first act of the play by the characters around him such as Antony: 'When Caesar says, "Do this", it is performed' (1.2.10). By comparison, Cassius emphasises the ordinary human nature of Caesar and asserts that his elevation is undeserved: 'Upon what meat doth this our Caesar feed / That he is grown so great? Age, thou art shamed!' (1.2.149–50). Caesar revels in his power, yet he is aware of the potential dangers of being in his position. He accurately perceives the envy and antagonism of Cassius towards him (1.2.192–5).

Caesar, on the one hand, is a practical man, not given to ready belief in prophecy or omens. He dismisses the Soothsayer's warning as the words of a dreamer, and ultimately ignores the misgivings of his wife, Calpurnia, who pleads with him not to venture forth to the Capitol. He is also unwilling to accept the interpretation of the augury that the sacrificed animal's missing heart is a warning for him (2.2.38–48). On the other hand, however, he is susceptible to some superstitions; he asks Antony to touch Calpurnia, in the course of the Lupercal celebrations, as a cure for her sterility (1.2.6–9).

Throughout the play there is a division between the conceptions of Caesar as a man and of him as the abstract ideal of a powerful ruler. Caesar often speaks of himself in the third person: 'Caesar shall forth' (2.2.10); 'Shall Caesar send a lie?' (2.2.65). This emphasises his understanding that, in addition to his ordinary self, he is a public entity with an image he needs to stage-manage. It is his careful concern for his public image that leads him to ignore the pleading of Calpurnia when Decius cunningly suggests, 'If Caesar hide himself, shall they not whisper, / "Lo, Caesar is afraid"?' (2.2.100–1).

The notion of the monarch as both a human being and an exalted ideal is explored across Shakespeare's work. Cassius expresses the frailty of Caesar to Brutus by relating how Caesar nearly drowned in the Tiber (the main river of Rome, 1.2.100–15). The public presentation of the body of Caesar, by Antony, also powerfully conveys the vulnerable humanity of the man. (Note Antony's powerful reference to Caesar as 'thou bleeding piece of earth', 3.1.254.) Yet paradoxically, after Caesar is dead, Brutus realises that they have only been able to kill his mortal body, while the spirit of Caesar lives on: 'O Julius Caesar, thou art mighty yet, / Thy spirit walks abroad and turns our swords / In our own proper entrails' (5.3.94–6). The political spirit, the abstract idea of the leader, has not been touched. Stage productions have sometimes used a prominent statue of Caesar as a prop to emphasise the enduring idea of

Caesar that persists beyond his death. The appearance of Caesar's ghost (4.3.275–86) also renders literal the endurance of the spirit of Caesar beyond his death.

Key point

Would Shakespeare's Caesar have accepted the crown, changing Rome from a republic to a monarchy, and was he a potential tyrant? These questions are unanswered in the play and Shakespeare infuses the issue with ambiguity. The account of Caesar being offered the crown three times and refusing it is given to Brutus, Cassius and the audience by Casca (1.2.220–43). Casca perceives Caesar as reluctant to relinquish the crown – 'to my thinking he was very loath to lay his fingers off it' (1.2.237–8) – but the audience is not shown the scene to make up its own mind on Caesar's response. It is also telling that when Brutus is debating the issue with himself his words describe possibilities, not certainties: 'he may do danger' (2.1.17); 'So Caesar may. / Then lest he may, prevent (2.1.27–8). Ultimately the conspirators act in anticipation of what Caesar might do, not in response to a certainty.

Mark Antony

Key quotes

Friends, Romans, countrymen, lend me your ears! (3.2.65)

A curse shall light upon the limbs of men:
Domestic fury and fierce civil strife
Shall cumber all the parts of Italy;
...
And Caesar's spirit, ranging for revenge,
With Ate by his side come hot from hell,
Shall in these confines with a monarch's voice
Cry havoc and let slip the dogs of war ... (3.1.262–4, 270–3)

Antony is a powerful ally of Caesar's. The conspirators are alert to this and debate whether to let him outlive the assassination (2.1.155–91). They make the mistake of letting Antony deliver a funeral oration to the crowd. Cassius accurately gauges the threat: 'Know you how much the people may be moved / By that which he will utter?' (3.1.234–5), but Brutus is blind to the risk and overrules him. Antony is intelligent, perceptive and a skilled orator. He accurately realises the power that the body of Caesar, with its multiple stab wounds, will have on the crowd. He imagines the wounds of Caesar as mouths which, although silent, will be eloquent in speaking: 'Over thy wounds now do I prophesy – / Which like dumb mouths do ope their ruby lips / To beg the voice and utterance of my tongue' (3.1.259–61). After his speech has roused the crowd to a fury, he is revealed as being highly conscious of the calculated effect of his words: 'Now let it work. Mischief, thou art afoot, / Take thou what course thou wilt!' (3.2.250–1).

Antony is pragmatic. Although he is distraught at the assassination, he is able to hide his feelings of antagonism towards the conspirators in the interests of his personal survival and in order to subsequently obtain his revenge. Once Caesar is dead, Antony becomes one of the triumvirs in a power sharing arrangement. His strong will is shown by his squabbles with Lepidus and Octavius (4.1) and his tussles on the battlefield with Octavius over who is giving the orders: 'Why do you cross me in this exigent?' (5.1.19). He is not willing to show Octavius the same deference he showed previously to Caesar.

Key point

There is a ruthless pragmatism to Antony. He has no qualms about agreeing to the death of his nephew (4.1.5–6), putting the needs of the state before emotional ties – paradoxically, a characteristic that Brutus shares. Shakespeare later presented a very different Antony in *Antony and Cleopatra* (c. 1606).

Minor characters

Portia and **Calpurnia** are significant minor characters in the play. In both ancient Rome and Elizabethan England, women did not have a say in government (the female monarch was the only exception). Women were generally consigned to the domestic sphere and were expected to be chaste, silent and obedient. Portia, the wife of Brutus, and Calpurnia, the wife of Caesar, only appear in private, domestic spaces. Both characters attempt to exert influence over their husbands but are ultimately unsuccessful. Portia, in order to persuade Brutus to see her as equal to the men around him and thus share his secrets with her, tries a range of strategies to overcome the narrow perception Brutus has of her: 'I have a man's mind, but a woman's might' (2.4.8). Calpurnia also attempts, in vain, to exert power over Caesar to protect him from the dangers waiting for him in the public sphere on the day of the assassination.

Many of the minor characters in the play have memorable and significant lines, such as the **Soothsayer** when he warns Caesar to 'Beware the Ides of March' (1.2.18). **Cicero**, a minor character with few lines, nevertheless makes an important point: 'men may construe things after their fashion / Clean from the purpose of the things themselves' (1.3.34–5), which resonates throughout the play where different viewpoints and interpretations of events have significant consequences. **Casca**, responding to Cassius' question about Cicero speaking Greek, 'To what effect?' (1.2.270), replies 'but for mine own part it was Greek to me' (1.2.273) – a comic reference meaning that he couldn't understand it. This expression is still familiar today.

The **plebeians** are significant minor characters, even though they are not given individual names and are only identified by occupation in the first scene. The major characters are constantly aware of, and place importance on, the view of the people: Brutus acts against Caesar in the (mistaken) belief that the people want him to, and both Brutus and Antony seek to persuade the people to view the assassination in particular ways. This gives the people a degree of political power, which would have been an intriguing concept for Shakespeare's audience. At the same time, the brutal death of Cinna the Poet presents the people as a frightening and irrational force.

THEMES, IDEAS & VALUES

Government

Key quotes

Liberty! Freedom! Tyranny is dead! (3.1.78)

Remember March, the Ides of March remember:
Did not great Julius bleed for justice' sake?
What villain touched his body, that did stab
And not for justice? (4.3.18–21)

O, what a fall was there, my countrymen!
Then I, and you, and all of us fell down,
Whilst bloody treason flourished over us. (3.2.181–3)

A central theme of the play is how power should be exercised. The conspirators go to great lengths to attempt to preserve the democracy of the Republic. Many of the ideas in the play would have been radical and challenging for Shakespeare's audience. In the Roman Republic, the common populace had a significantly greater say in how they were governed than Elizabethans could ever have hoped for. Early modern society was highly hierarchical; power was concentrated in the monarch, who generally obtained the crown by hereditary right, and to a lesser extent in the nobility. There was no process of democratic election. Ordinary people had no say in how they were governed and rebellion was highly risky, generally resulting in execution. A play such as *Julius Caesar* gave the theatre audience insights into political ideas, motivations and discussions that were not a part of its ordinary experience. The theatre was a powerful political space where ideas could be expressed and explored.

Julius Caesar is a story of political rebellion and its consequences. The fact that the play was set in Rome, rather than England, allowed the playwright to explore ideas that would otherwise be risky. The Roman setting and the historical sources enabled a certain degree of freedom for

Shakespeare to explore issues that were potentially explosive. The play is also powerful in its presentation of alternative government systems. *Julius Caesar* presents a clash between different ideals of political power. By presenting alternatives, and the way in which there were changes to a political system in the history of Rome, the play implicitly challenges Elizabethan ideas of monarchy as the only valid system of government.

It is interesting to consider what happens in the aftermath of the assassination, an event that was intended to preserve the ideals of the Roman Republic. With the removal of Caesar, power is shared, yet divisions and tensions quickly appear; Rome degenerates into civil war and the ordinary people manifest irrational brutality. (You may want to consider the excesses in the aftermath of the French Revolution and compare them with how Shakespeare perceives some of the consequences of political change.)

Key point

Consider how the senators, in their excessive reverence to Caesar at the beginning of the play, contribute to the potential for Caesar's position to be abused. Leaders are unable to create their positions alone; they require the agreement of many to achieve their status. Shakespeare, across his tragedy and history plays, was deeply interested in the complexities of political power.

Rhetoric

Key quotes

I can o'ersway him, for he loves to hear
That unicorns may be betrayed with trees,
And bears with glasses, elephants with holes,
Lions with toils, and men with flatterers.
But when I tell him he hates flatterers
He says he does, being then most flatterèd.
Let me work:
For I can give his humour the true bent,
And I will bring him to the Capitol. (2.1.203–11)

The power of speech is an important theme in the play. Oratory (public speaking) was an important and well-respected practice in ancient Rome and also in Shakespeare's England. In their orations, the characters use rhetoric. The classical writer Plato, in his work *The Republic* (c. 375 BC), observed that rhetoric 'is a producer of persuasion for belief, not for instruction in the matter of right and wrong' (455a). The object of rhetoric is to persuade an audience to a certain belief. The fact that the Roman crowd (and the theatre audience) is moved firstly by Brutus and then by Antony suggests two things: the changeability of the crowd (and us), and the power of language. The conflict created suggests the extent to which language can create perceptions and alter how we view reality. Brutus attempts to make the assassination a sacred and noble act, but does his rhetoric ultimately fail to transform reality? Alternatively, we could say that different characters use language to create different 'realities' of the same event.

Different characters throughout the play wield the power of persuasion. Brutus is moved to act by Cassius, who manipulates him by deceptively making it appear that many people, not just Cassius himself, want him to act against Caesar. After Caesar's death we see Brutus and Antony move the crowd through their words; how the crowd perceives the death of Caesar depends on the rhetorical power of the speakers. Other characters also attempt to persuade by their rhetoric. Caesar's wife, Calpurnia, attempts to dissuade him from venturing forth on the fatal day. At first Caesar seems to be swayed by her pleas, but he is then moved by Decius' words to go to the Capitol. Portia attempts to persuade her husband to share his thoughts and plans with her. Both wives are unsuccessful in exercising their powers of persuasion; their husbands ignore them, to their own detriment.

Key point

Part of Shakespeare's education involved having to argue, often in Latin, one proposal, and then the opposite. He was thus highly attuned to the power of language and argument, and skilled in the ability to see an event or idea from different perspectives.

Honour

Key quotes

Set honour in one eye and death i'th'other
And I will look on both indifferently.
For let the gods so speed me as I love
The name of honour more than I fear death. (1.2.86–9)

For Brutus is an honourable man,
So are they all, all honourable men – (3.2.74–5)

Honour was a key value that Shakespeare and his contemporaries associated with the ancient Romans. Honour involved a sense of self-sacrifice and of acting for the good of others. It also meant acting in accordance with certain ideals and standards. Brutus is a key character associated with honour in the play. When Cassius first begins to suggest to Brutus that he should act in response to Caesar's growing ambition, Brutus appears only open to acting if it is 'toward the general good' (1.2.85). Brutus is only able to act against Caesar because he perceives, or at least frames, the assassination as an honourable act to uphold the ideals of the Roman Republic. Brutus has a strong sense of history and sees himself as acting on behalf of Rome.

Suicide, although a sin for early modern Christians, was strongly associated with the Roman value of honour in the face of defeat. It was perceived as an act that responded to a character's sense of shame, akin to revenge against the self for some perceived failing or shortcoming. Although our contemporary views on suicide generally perceive it as tragic and misguided, for ancient Romans it was a dignified act of courage. Before committing suicide, Cassius castigates himself for not acting sooner: 'O, coward that I am to live so long / To see my best friend ta'en before my face' (5.3.34–5). His follower Titinius soon follows suit, observing 'This is a Roman's part' (5.3.89). Earlier in the play, when Brutus was justifying his actions in his funeral oration to the crowd, he claimed that he would be as ready to kill himself for Rome as he was prepared to kill Caesar: 'as I slew my best lover for the good of Rome, I have the same dagger for myself when it shall please my country to need my death' (3.2.38–9).

Key point

Note the responses by other characters to Brutus' death. Strato observes that in killing himself, 'Brutus only overcame himself, / And no man else hath honour by his death' (5.5.56–7), to which Lucilius replies: 'So Brutus should be found' (5.5.58). Earlier Lucilius had predicted that Brutus would not be killed by anyone else: 'I dare assure thee that no enemy / Shall ever take alive the noble Brutus. / The gods defend him from so great a shame!' (5.4.21–3). They perceive Brutus as too honourable to have been taken by his enemies. Brutus committing suicide is consistent with his character and how he acts throughout the play.

Fate, prophecy and the supernatural

Key quotes

But if you would consider the true cause
Why all these fires, why all these gliding ghosts,
Why birds and beasts from quality and kind,
Why old men, fools, and children calculate,
Why all these things change from their ordinance,
Their natures, and preformèd faculties,
To monstrous quality – why, you shall find
That heaven hath infused them with these spirits
To make them instruments of fear, and warning
Unto some monstrous state. (1.3.62–71)

Yet now they fright me. There is one within,
Besides the things that we have heard and seen,
Recounts most horrid sights seen by the watch.
A lioness hath whelpèd in the streets,
And graves have yawned and yielded up their dead;
Fierce fiery warriors fight upon the clouds
In ranks and squadrons and right form of war,
Which drizzled blood upon the Capitol;
The noise of battle hurtled in the air,
Horses did neigh and dying men did groan,
And ghosts did shriek and squeal about the streets. (2.2.14–24)

As well as the fierce storm that arises in 1.3, several characters report various supernatural events prior to the assassination. These suggest that something is about to occur that is contrary to the natural order. In Elizabethan England, the killing of a supposedly divinely ordained monarch would generally have been seen as an act against God's will. (In the mid seventeenth century, many perceived the beheading of King Charles I as contrary to God's will.) When Casca reports to Cicero the storm and strange events occurring, he observes that: 'Either there is a civil strife in heaven, / Or else the world, too saucy with the gods, / Incenses them to send destruction' (1.3.11–13). He suggests that disturbances in nature reflect the anger of the gods; however, Cicero reminds him that all events are subject to different interpretations: 'But men may construe things after their fashion / Clean from the purpose of the things themselves' (1.3.34–5).

It is interesting to note that the impending death of Caesar is being treated in the play, from one perspective, as if he were a monarch. When Calpurnia expresses her fears to Caesar, he tries to allay them, saying 'these predictions / Are to the world in general as to Caesar' (2.2.28–9); however, Calpurnia replies 'When beggars die there are no comets seen, / The heavens themselves blaze forth the death of princes' (2.2.30–1). She suggests that nature, and by implication the gods that control and communicate through nature, only responds to the deaths of those with the highest rank in society.

Key point

There is a paradox within these supernatural events. The events, such as the opening graves (2.2.18) and raining fire (1.3.10), suggest that the assassination is somehow contrary to the natural order. At the same time, the accurate prophecy of the Soothsayer and Calpurnia's dreams that predict the death of Caesar (and mode of death: 'She dreamt tonight she saw my statue, / Which like a fountain with an hundred spouts / Did run pure blood', 2.2.76–8) suggest that events are predestined and able to be seen ahead of time by some, implying an overall order to history.

Loyalty

Key quotes

> For Brutus, as you know, was Caesar's angel.
> Judge, O you gods, how dearly Caesar loved him!
> This was the most unkindest cut of all. (3.2.172–4)

In Shakespeare's hierarchical society, obedience, of servants towards masters, wives towards husbands, the lower class to the nobility, and subjects to their monarch, was a primary method of social control and of central importance to those in positions of power. The rigid structures of society depended on people accepting their social position and not challenging those structures. Shakespeare, in many of his plays, is interested in exploring the limits of obedience and loyalty. His interest in Brutus is based on the premise that Brutus is essentially a good man faced with an untenable situation: the potential abuse of power that threatens Roman government. Yet Caesar is also good friends with Brutus. To whom should Brutus be loyal: Caesar or Rome?

There are other relationships that are tested in different ways. Brutus and Cassius have a close bond, yet that bond is tested in 4.2 and 4.3 when Brutus accuses Cassius of taking bribes and thus sullying their reputation as honourable and virtuous. Brutus sees Cassius as being disloyal by contaminating the justice of their cause with base corruption (4.3.18–28). Likewise, Cassius sees Brutus as being disloyal to their friendship: 'You wrong me every way, you wrong me, Brutus' (4.3.55).

Key point

Loyalty can be deadly. Cassius commits suicide because he cannot bear the thought of Brutus being taken by the enemy (5.3.34–46), and Titinius commits suicide out of loyalty to Cassius (5.3.87–90). Brutus and Cassius ask their followers to demonstrate their loyalty by assisting their masters to die. Cassius asks Pindarus to stab him (5.3.40–5) and Strato agrees to assist Brutus' suicide, although Clitus, Dardanius and Volumnius refuse (5.5.47–50).

History and performance

Key quotes

So often shall the knot of us be called
The men that gave their country liberty. (3.1.117–18)

How many ages hence
Shall this our lofty scene be acted over
In states unborn and accents yet unknown! (3.1.111–13)

Some points in the play reflect a degree of self-consciousness about the fact that, in one sense, it is a performance of history. For example, the conspirators show awareness that the assassination is an event that will be replayed in the future. Brutus asks 'How many times shall Caesar bleed in sport' (3.1.114), imagining how their act will become theatre. The murder can therefore be thought of as a form of theatre, the first of many performances. At the same time, the observation reminds the audience that they are watching a play, momentarily lifting them out from their immersion in the illusion of the performance. Where speeches or events in plays draw attention to the process of theatrical performance itself, this is referred to as metatheatrical or metadramatic.

Key point

The reflection that the assassination will be replayed frequently in the future also conveys Shakespeare's awareness that his art had the potential to endure. By reflecting on how an ancient story had survived into the sixteenth century, he was aware that his stories, too, had the potential to travel into the future.

DIFFERENT INTERPRETATIONS

Different interpretations arise from different responses to a text. Over time, a text will evoke a wide range of responses from its readers, who may come from various social or cultural groups and live in very different places and historical periods. These responses can be published in newspapers, journals and books by critics and reviewers, or they can be expressed in discussions among readers in classrooms, book groups, the media and so on. While there is no single correct reading of a text, it is important to understand that an interpretation is more than a personal opinion – it is the justification of a point of view on the text. To present an interpretation of the text based on your point of view you must use a logical argument and support it with relevant evidence from the text.

The critics' viewpoints

Since Shakespeare's work has been around for a long time, there is a substantial amount of critical material about his plays and poetry. This can be daunting for students and critics alike. Whether you are expected to research some literary criticism as part of your study will depend on your level and the expectations of your teacher. If you do need to do this, keep in mind that it is not possible for anyone to read and understand everything that is relevant to the play. Try to select a few articles or book sections that discuss an area of interest to you. Reading literary criticism should be enjoyable and is intended to help you order your thoughts and shape your own ideas about the play. It can also open your eyes to aspects of the play that you hadn't noticed before.

In trying to gain an overall sense of the literary criticism relevant to *Julius Caesar*, a useful place to start is with a few scholarly editions of the play that provide an overview of the different approaches taken by critics. For example, you could look at the outlines by Martin Spevack and Marga Munkelt in the New Cambridge Shakespeare edition of

Julius Caesar (2003) and David Daniell's introduction to the Arden Shakespeare edition (1998), each of which has an appendix with useful excerpts from Plutarch's *Lives of the Noble Grecians and Romanes* (the translation by Thomas North 1579), which is a primary source for Shakespeare.

It is also helpful to look at edited collections of essays so that you gain a sense of some different perspectives on the play, rather than just one critic's viewpoint. A good example is Horst Zander's *Julius Caesar: New Critical Essays* (2005). Essay collections are also valuable when a critic looks at different aspects and themes of the play, such as in Mary Hamer's *William Shakespeare, Julius Caesar* (1998). Hamer considers themes such as Shakespeare's engagement with history, aspects of violence, Portia and Calpurnia and the position of women generally, as well as the role of men and ideas of what it is to be 'Roman'. Also useful are Jo McMurtry's *Julius Caesar: A Guide to the Play* (1998) and Vivian Thomas's *Julius Caesar* (1992).

Since Shakespeare has several plays (*Titus Andronicus, Coriolanus, Julius Caesar* and *Antony and Cleopatra*) and a poem (*The Rape of Lucrece*) set in Rome, you may wish to think about how Shakespeare imagined Rome in his work and what values he, and the early modern period generally, associated with Rome. Warren Chernaik's *The Myth of Rome* (2011) is an excellent starting point. The chapter on *Julius Caesar* places the play in various contexts, considering how Caesar has been viewed throughout history and how other early modern playwrights represented Caesar, and provides many valuable insights on the play. Also see Derek Traversi's *Shakespeare: the Roman Plays* (1963) and Barbara Parker's 2005 essay 'From Monarchy to Tyranny: Julius Caesar among Shakespeare's Roman works'. Geoffrey Miles considers the character of Brutus in the context of the philosophy of Stoicism in *Shakespeare and the Constant Romans* (1996). Also, an invaluable reference guide to all aspects of classical culture is *The Oxford Companion to Classical Literature, 2nd ed.* (1997) edited by MC Howatson.

It is also often useful to read a work that looks at aspects of the early modern or classical culture that Shakespeare's play reflects. For example Ian Munro, in his study *The Figure of the Crowd in Early Modern London: The City and its Double* (2005), explores the links between dramatic space, such as the relationship between the crowd in *Julius Caesar* and the theatre audience. Also see Annabel Patterson's *Shakespeare and the Popular Voice* (1989). For some historical contexts on suicide see Dominique Goy-Blanquet's article '"Death of liberty": the fashion in shrouds' (1990).

One of the issues that critics often explore is how Shakespeare responded to his historical sources. Vivian Thomas' essay 'Shakespeare's Sources: Translations, Transformations, and Intertextuality' (2005) is excellent in this regard. Martin Jehne (2005) considers the play's relationship with different historical ideas about who Julius Caesar was, while Clifford Ronan (2005) situates Shakespeare's play within the context of other early modern dramatic representations of Caesar. Also see Robert Miola's article, 'Shakespeare and his Sources: Observations on the Critical History of *Julius Caesar*' (1987). Some critics explore how the politics of the Roman world was relevant to Shakespeare's time; for example, Claudia Corti argues that the play was directed at Elizabeth I and intended as a warning against tyranny (1999).

Language, rhetoric and the power of speech are significant aspects of the play that have been explored. John McClelland analyses the speeches given in the forum by Brutus and Antony in his essay 'Text, rhetoric, meaning' (1987); also refer to Bryan Loughrey's essay '"I am no orator": the language of public spaces' (1992) and Jean Fuzier's 'Rhetoric Versus Rhetoric: A Study of Shakespeare's *Julius Caesar*, Act III, Scene 2' (1974). In 'The Power of Speech / To Stir Men's Blood', Gayle Greene observes how in the play 'language is power and characters rise or fall on the basis of their ability to wield words' (1980, p.68). Maurice Charney, in *Shakespeare's Roman Plays: The Function of Imagery in the Drama* (1961), explores the imagery of *Julius Caesar*, observing that the significant images of the play are blood and fire. For commentary on the play's structure see John Velz's article 'Undular Structure in *Julius Caesar*' (1971).

For studies on the female characters of the play, women across Shakespeare's Roman plays and gender issues generally, see Naomi Conn Liebler's 'What Portia knew' (1998), Gail Kern Paster's ' "In the spirit of men there is no blood": Blood as trope of gender in *Julius Caesar*' (1989) and Coppélia Kahn's *Roman Shakespeare: Warriors, Wounds, and Women* (1997).

For surveys and commentary on the film versions of *Julius Caesar* see Munkelt's summary in the New Cambridge edition (Spevack 2003, pp.69–70), Zander in *Julius Caesar: New Critical Essays* (2005, pp.41–5), Rothwell and Melzer in *Shakespeare on Screen* (pp.112–26) and Brode's essay 'A tide in men's lives: *Julius Caesar*' in *Shakespeare in the Movies* (2000). For analyses of particular films and a complete film bibliography see the essay collection *Shakespeare on Screen: The Roman Plays* edited by Sarah Hatchuel and Nathalie Vienne-Guerrin (2009).

Two contrasting interpretations

Any text is open to contrasting, yet equally valid, interpretations. Here are two different arguments on how the play presents the validity of the actions of the conspirators.

1 The play presents the assassination of Caesar as a justifiable act attempting to preserve the ideal of democracy in Rome.

In *Julius Caesar* the growing power of Caesar threatens the Roman Republic. What is at stake is not simply a transfer in authority between rulers but a dangerous shift in the *type* of government that controls Rome and the way in which power is exercised. Shakespeare conveys this threat in his depiction of Caesar and the way individuals act towards him. His demands are automatically met and his will is not questioned. There is a real risk that Caesar will accept the crown and become a monarch; the account by Casca conveys how Caesar was increasingly reluctant to let the crown go each time it was offered (1.2.233–44). Caesar is portrayed as arrogant; when he tells Decius that he will not go to the Capitol and Decius asks for a reason, Caesar replies 'The cause is in my will' (2.2.71). Caesar sees himself as above the need to justify his actions to anyone.

Shakespeare conveys the legitimacy of the assassination by presenting Brutus, the dominant figure of the group of conspirators, as a noble, honourable citizen whose concern is for the Roman Republic. He does not act selfishly but for the common good. Even the enemies of Brutus recognise this. As Antony observes:

> This was the noblest Roman of them all:
> All the conspirators, save only he,
> Did that they did in envy of great Caesar.
> He only, in a general honest thought
> And common good to all, made one of them. (5.5.68–72)

The high standing of Brutus among his friends, followers and enemies alike, has the effect of casting the killing of Caesar in a virtuous light; it suggests that the assassination was not a base deed carried out for selfish motives. When Brutus dies he observes: 'Caesar, now be still, / I killed not thee with half so good a will' (5.5.50–1), which conveys his reluctance to kill Caesar. The play suggests that the assassination was a difficult decision, but a justifiable and legitimate one; what was at stake was nothing less than the ideal of Rome itself.

2 The play ultimately suggests that the assassination of Julius Caesar was wrongful and unlawful.

Although Brutus attempts to frame the assassination as an honourable act carried out for the good of Rome, Shakespeare's language constantly undermines this idea. Antony's powerful imagery of the hunt, which imagines Caesar as 'like a deer strucken by many princes' (3.1.209), reduces the act to the level of animal savagery. The scene of the conspirators washing their hands in the blood of Caesar is disturbingly macabre and Brutus' lofty idealism is brought down to earth by Antony's funeral oration, which draws attention to the brutal reality of the deed.

The legitimacy of the conspiracy is undermined from the beginning through Shakespeare's depiction of Cassius as manipulative and sly. Aware that Brutus will only be moved to act if he sees himself as acting on behalf of the people, Cassius orchestrates forged notes to be left for Brutus to find; Brutus is stirred to act partly on the basis of an erroneous belief that the people wish him to act. While Brutus is depicted as noble and honourable, if misguided, those around him are not so pure. Brutus is furious that Cassius has 'an itching palm' (4.3.10), compromising their side's public image. Brutus, in anger, says 'Did not great Julius bleed for justice' sake?' (4.3.19), as he confronts the reality that those around him do not live up to his own standards.

The play's structure also suggests that the assassination is wrong. Caesar is assassinated relatively early in the play in 3.1, yet the drama continues for another two acts to play out the consequences of the deed. What comes of the bloody deed? Civil war and chaos – in killing Caesar, the conspirators do not liberate Rome from tyranny and restore democracy. In any event, the play does not present the plebeians as capable of rational use of democratic power. In the wake of the assassination, the ordinary Romans are not grateful to the conspirators; instead they are wrathful, vengeful and irrational, brutally killing Cinna the Poet in a chilling scene of mob violence.

By the end of the play, Caesar's murder appears misguided and all in vain. When Cassius and Brutus die, they construct their own deaths as revenge by Caesar: Cassius observes 'Caesar, thou art revenged' (5.3.45) and Brutus says 'Caesar, now be still' (5.5.50). Thus the play seems to present the conspirators as paying with their lives for the wrongful act of the assassination.

QUESTIONS & ANSWERS

This section focuses on your own analytical writing on the text, and gives you strategies for producing high-quality responses in your coursework and exam essays.

Essay writing – an overview

An essay is a formal and serious piece of writing that presents your point of view on the text, usually in response to a given essay topic. Your 'point of view' in an essay is your interpretation of the meaning of the text's language, structure, characters, situations and events, supported by detailed analysis of textual evidence.

Analyse – don't summarise

In your essays it is important to avoid simply summarising what happens in a text:

- A **summary** is a description or paraphrase (retelling in different words) of the characters and events. For example: 'Macbeth has a horrifying vision of a dagger dripping with blood before he goes to murder King Duncan'.
- An **analysis** is an explanation of the real meaning or significance that lies 'beneath' the text's words (and images, for a film). For example: 'Macbeth's vision of a bloody dagger shows how deeply uneasy he is about the violent act he is contemplating – as well as his sense that supernatural forces are impelling him to act'.

A limited amount of summary is sometimes necessary to let your reader know which part of the text you wish to discuss. However, always keep this to a minimum and follow it immediately with your analysis (explanation) of what this part of the text is really telling us.

Plan your essay

Carefully plan your essay so that you have a clear idea of what you are going to say. The plan ensures that your ideas flow logically, that your argument remains consistent and that you stay on the topic. An essay plan should be a list of **brief dot points** – no more than half a page.

- Include your central argument or main contention – a concise statement of your overall response to the topic.
- Write three or four dot points for each paragraph, indicating the main idea and evidence/examples from the text. Note that in your essay you will need to *expand* on these points and *analyse* the evidence.

Structure your essay

An essay is a complete, self-contained piece of writing. It has a clear beginning (the introduction), middle (several body paragraphs) and end (the last paragraph or conclusion). It must also have a central argument that runs throughout, linking each paragraph to form a coherent whole.

See examples of introductions and conclusions in the 'Sample analysis of a topic' and 'Sample answer' sections.

The introduction establishes your overall response to the topic. It includes your main contention and outlines the main evidence you will refer to in the course of the essay. Write your introduction *after* you have done a plan and *before* you write the rest of the essay.

The body paragraphs argue your case – they present evidence from the text and explain how this evidence supports your argument. Each body paragraph needs:

- a strong **topic sentence** (usually the first sentence) that states the main point being made in the paragraph
- **evidence** from the text, including some brief quotations
- **analysis** of the textual evidence explaining its significance and how it supports your argument
- **links back to the topic** in one or more statements, usually towards the end of the paragraph.

Connect the body paragraphs so that your discussion flows smoothly. Use some linking words and phrases like 'similarly' and 'on the other hand', though don't start every paragraph like this. Another strategy is to use a significant word from the last sentence of one paragraph in the first sentence of the next.

Use key terms from the topic – or synonyms for them – throughout, so the relevance of your discussion to the topic is always clear.

The conclusion ties everything together and finishes the essay. It includes strong statements that emphasise your central argument and provide a clear response to the topic.

Avoid simply restating the points made earlier in the essay – this will end your essay on a very flat note and imply that you have run out of ideas and vocabulary. The conclusion is meant to be a logical extension of what you have written, not just a repetition or summary of it. Writing an effective conclusion can be a challenge. Try using these tips:

- Start by linking back to the final sentence of the second-last paragraph rather than just leaping back to your main contention straight away – this helps your writing to 'flow'.
- Use synonyms and expressions with equivalent meanings to vary your vocabulary. This allows you to reinforce your line of argument without being repetitive.
- When planning your essay, think of one or two broad statements or observations about the text's wider meaning. These should be related to the topic and your overall argument. Keep them for the conclusion, since they will give you something 'new' to say but still follow logically from your discussion. The introduction will be focused on the topic, but the conclusion can present a wider view of the text.

Essay topics

1 Discuss the power of rhetoric (persuasive speech) in the play. Consider how Cassius persuades Brutus to act against Caesar, how Brutus and Antony persuade the crowd, and how Calpurnia and Portia attempt to persuade their husbands to act in certain ways.

2 *Julius Caesar* makes extensive references to omens, premonitions and other aspects of the supernatural. Discuss the effect and function of these in the play, analysing various examples from the text.

3 What does the play suggest about how society should be governed and what the responsibilities of citizens should be? Find examples from the play where characters express political ideas.

4 Analyse the character of Brutus. How does Shakespeare present him? What changes does Brutus undergo in the course of the play?

5 What ideas does the play present about Romans and Roman beliefs and customs? What values, virtues and flaws are associated with Roman society?

6 Discuss ideas of loyalty and obedience to people or to the political state. Who owes duties to whom, and how are these upheld or transgressed?

7 Discuss ideas of gender in the play. How are women portrayed and what assumptions underlie these depictions? Use examples from the text to support your arguments.

8 *Julius Caesar* is classified as a tragedy but is analogous to a history play. Discuss aspects of the play that align it with both genres.

9 Discuss the presentation of violence and death in the play. If you were a theatre or film director, how would you stage or film some of the key scenes of *Julius Caesar*? You may wish to consider the following: how you would position the actors, what settings and costumes you would use, what camera angles and use of close-up shots would be most effective, and what gestures and emotions you would ask your actors to convey.

10 *Julius Caesar* is a play that draws from historical events. What issues and problems arise from this? How has Shakespeare responded to these challenges?

Useful vocabulary for writing on *Julius Caesar*

This section includes a list of words you might find useful when writing about the play and literary or dramatic works generally. Also note that when you refer to a line from the play you will generally be asked to use numbers that refer to the act, scene and line. So, for example, 2.4.10 means Act 2, Scene 4, line 10.

Act: a major division in a play; in *Julius Caesar* there are five acts.

Blank verse: plain verse with no rhyming words at the end of the lines.

Character: a fictional person in a literary or dramatic work.

Dramatic irony: when the audience knows something that a character does not.

Elizabethan: the period from 1558 to 1603, in which Elizabeth I was on the throne; *Julius Caesar* was thus written in the Elizabethan period. Plays written after her death in 1603, when James I became king, fall into the Jacobean period.

Foreshadowing: an idea, event or image within a literary or dramatic work that indicates that an event will occur later in the narrative.

Genre: a category of literary or dramatic work with a set of conventions (rules) that determine the characteristics of that type of work; examples include comedy, tragedy and history.

Historical context: aspects of the society and culture of the period and the place in which a text was produced that may be relevant to take into account when reading it. This may include events, attitudes, other texts, behaviours, objects, beliefs and values.

Iambic pentameter: where a line of verse has the stresses (beats) falling on every second syllable (iambic), and there are five stresses to a line (pentameter), totalling ten syllables.

Metaphor: a word or phrase used to describe something by comparing it to something else; the word in Greek meant 'carrying from one place to another'.

Oratory: public speaking; the practical application of the theoretical art of speaking (rhetoric).

Oxymoron: contradictory terms used in conjunction.

Patricians: the upper class of Rome; members of privileged families.

Personification: a figure of speech where an abstract idea, inanimate object or animal is given human characteristics.

Plebeians: the common people of Rome.

Renaissance: the term 'Renaissance' in relation to English literature is the period from the late sixteenth century up until 1660. Shakespeare was writing in the English Renaissance period.

Rhyming couplet: two lines of verse, the last words of which rhyme.

Rhetoric: the theoretical art of speaking; persuasive speech.

Senate: the council and law-making body of Rome; generally senators tended to be from rich families and membership was hereditary.

Simile: similar to a metaphor but using the words 'as' or 'like'; for example, 'As huge as high Olympus' (4.3.92).

Soliloquy: a dramatic speech spoken by a single character, usually when alone on the stage.

Sonnet: a verse comprising fourteen lines with a specific rhyming pattern (rhyming couplets or other combinations).

Stage direction: a note in the text of a play that tells actors what to do; generally minimal in the Elizabethan and Jacobean periods.

Stoicism: a Greek philosophical school that emphasised constancy, bravery and self-sufficiency in the face of misfortune; Shakespeare and his contemporaries associated the Romans with Stoic virtues.

Tragedy: a particular genre of drama, originating in Greece, comprising events of misfortune and ending with the deaths of multiple characters including the principal characters who traditionally are of high social status and power.

Sample analysis of a topic

Julius Caesar **is a play that explores the power of rhetoric. Discuss the different ways in the play that characters are persuaded to act.**

Sample introduction

Julius Caesar explores the power of rhetoric. Many of the characters seek to convince others to act in certain ways through powerful and persuasive speech. Characters are able to induce others to take particular courses of action or hold particular beliefs and thus effect momentous change through the power of persuasive speech. This essay will examine how different characters use rhetoric and how Shakespeare, through his presentation of equally forceful alternative perspectives on events and actions, explores the elusive nature of truth.

Paragraph outline

Body paragraph 1: Cassius persuading Brutus

Topic sentence: Before Brutus resolves to act against Caesar, he is manipulated by Cassius into believing that many Romans regard him highly and desire him to act. Consider the characters of Brutus and Cassius and find examples of what Cassius says and does to move Brutus. The deception of Cassius is important since it has the effect of undermining the apparent virtue and nobility of the assassination, so try to draw out some points in this regard.

Body paragraph 2: Husbands and wives

Topic sentence: Women in the play are presented as particularly unsuccessful in using their speech to persuade. Look at the scenes of Portia attempting to persuade Brutus to take her into his confidence, and then look at Calpurnia trying to dissuade Caesar from venturing forth to the Capitol. Select some quotations and comment on what effect is created by the failure of the women to persuade their husbands to act in certain ways. Explain what assumptions underlie this failure and outline historical contexts relevant to the position of women.

Body paragraph 3: Moving the crowd

Topic sentence: Throughout the play, the crowd, the group of ordinary Romans, is a significant force. Many characters are highly conscious of the way the people will respond to events and contrive to seek their approval. Examine the scene of the competing funeral orations and find some relevant quotations relating to how the speakers seek to sway the crowd to agree with them. Think about how Shakespeare's audience would have responded to the idea that the crowd's opinion was thought valuable. Also consider parallels between the Roman crowd depicted on the stage and the actual audience watching the play.

Sample conclusion

This essay has explored the power of rhetoric in *Julius Caesar* and the different ways characters, with varying degrees of success, seek to persuade others to act. The effect of this is to make uncertain any ideas of 'truth' and 'reality'. What emerges is that our opinions often depend on the stories we tell ourselves and others, and on the persuasive ways stories are narrated. This was a powerful, and in many ways a particularly modern, concept that Shakespeare presents throughout his work. It renders the play compelling, while also maintaining contemporary relevance in our modern era of mass communication and sophisticated media technologies.

SAMPLE ANSWER

***Julius Caesar* presents political ideas that were radical and challenging for Shakespeare's audience. Discuss.**

Shakespeare's *Julius Caesar* is a play that explores various political ideas that would have been particularly radical and challenging for his audiences. This essay will outline how these ideas are presented in the play and the historical contexts that would have affected how they were received by Shakespeare's audience. I will argue that Shakespeare constructs his play in order to present different perspectives on how power should be exercised in society and the consequences of violent rebellion.

Julius Caesar depicts a violent attempt to preserve the Roman Republic and explores the consequences of the assassination of Caesar. The play is set at the end of the period of the Roman Republic, when the system of government was a form of democracy. Although many sectors of society, such as women and non-citizens (slaves and former slaves), did not have a say in government, male citizens, represented by tribunes, had some limited powers. The senators, drawn from the patricians (the upper classes), were elected to the senate. It is this political system that Brutus, Cassius and the conspirators see as threatened by the growing power of Caesar. As Brutus observes, 'Shall Rome stand under one man's awe?' (2.1.52). In the first act, Caesar is offered the crown (1.2.233–44) and although he refuses, there is a risk that a complete shift in the system of government is imminent: 'I do fear the people / Choose Caesar for their king' (Brutus 1.2.79–80). If Caesar were to accept the crown and become king, democracy in Rome would end; there would be no elected positions and Caesar's power would pass to his heirs by birthright, not merit.

The Republic that Brutus and the others try to preserve would have presented a radical and challenging idea to Shakespeare's audience because Elizabethan England was a monarchy. All power was vested in Elizabeth I and the crown passed according to hereditary right. There were no elected positions of power; the monarch made all political appointments. Furthermore, the monarch ruled by reason of divine right and was, in theory, God's appointed representative on earth. When Caesar acts and is treated like a god – 'When Caesar says, "Do this", it is performed' (Antony 1.2.10) – such a response to a leader's command would have been familiar to Shakespeare's audience. What would not have been familiar (or at least not officially recognised) is the horror and unease that this behaviour provokes in Brutus and the conspirators. Cassius voices ideas that some Elizabethans may have felt privately about their monarch but could not express publicly – namely, that Caesar as a person was as vulnerable as any other: 'He had a fever when he was in Spain, / And when the fit was on him I did mark / How he did shake. 'Tis true, this god did shake' (1.2.119–21).

Shakespeare presents different viewpoints on these challenging political ideas. On the one hand, the play provides a dramatic vehicle to express the radical concept of rebellion, and the idea that a leader with absolute power is dangerous and wrong. The conspirators challenge the idea of Caesar as an absolute ruler: 'The fault, dear Brutus, is not in our stars / But in ourselves, that we are underlings' (1.2.140–1). At the same time, Shakespeare also presents the opposing viewpoint. The conspiracy fails to kill the spirit of Caesar, the idea of the absolute ruler: 'O Julius Caesar, thou art mighty yet, / Thy spirit walks abroad and turns our swords / In our own proper entrails' (5.3.94–6). Furthermore, the assassination precipitates Rome's descent into chaos and civil war, leading ultimately, as Shakespeare's audience knew, to the establishment of the Roman Empire with Octavian (Augustus) as the first emperor.

By setting the play in ancient Rome, and drawing from well-known historical events, Shakespeare was able to present these challenging political ideas without risk of incurring censure. The polyvocal nature of his play, with its multiple perspectives, was a further protection in dealing with potentially explosive material, and added complexity and interest to the subject matter. The assassination represents both 'Liberty!' and 'Freedom!' (3.1.78) and, at the same time, 'bloody treason' (3.2.183). The conspirators are both liberators and 'brutish beasts' (3.2.96).

Finally, and perhaps most radically, *Julius Caesar* is a play where the ordinary person's opinion has a powerful political force. Brutus and Antony strive to sway the plebeians to their point of view in 3.2. Brutus knows that the conspirators must appease the multitude (3.1.179–80); Antony says that he will 'try / In my oration how the people take / The cruel issue of these bloody men' (3.1.292–4). Again Shakespeare presents the ordinary Romans from different perspectives; Casca is derisive of their 'sweaty nightcaps' and 'stinking breath' (1.2.241) and in the brutal killing of Cinna the Poet the mob is depicted as violent and irrational. Yet throughout the play there is a constant awareness that the opinion of the people matters. This powerful idea would have been of intense interest to Shakespeare's audience, in a society where the ordinary Elizabethan had no say and no political power. Modern productions of the play, which have alluded to fascism and various dictatorships through costume and setting, continue to render *Julius Caesar* a powerful political play that challenges tyranny.

REFERENCES & READING

Texts

Spevack, M (ed.) 2003, *Julius Caesar*, Cambridge University Press, The New Cambridge Shakespeare, Cambridge.

References

Brode, D 2000 'A tide in men's lives: *Julius Caesar*' in *Shakespeare in the Movies: From the Silent Era to Shakespeare in Love*, Oxford University Press, New York.

Charney, M 1961, *Shakespeare's Roman Plays: The Function of Imagery in the Drama*, Harvard University Press, Cambridge (Mass.).

Chernaik, W 2011, *The Myth of Rome in Shakespeare and His Contemporaries*, Cambridge University Press, Cambridge.

Corti, C 1999, 'Shakespeare's uncultured Caesar on the Elizabethan stage', in M Marrapodi and G Melchiori, eds, *Italian Studies in Shakespeare and His Contemporaries*, University of Delaware Press & Associated University Presses, Newark & London, pp.109–27.

Daniell, D (ed.) 1998, *Julius Caesar*, The Arden Shakespeare, Bloomsbury, London.

Fuzier, J 1974, 'Rhetoric Versus Rhetoric: A Study of Shakespeare's *Julius Caesar*, Act III, Scene 2', *Cahiers Elisabethains*, 5, pp.25–65.

Goy-Blanquet, D 1990, '"Death of liberty": the fashion in shrouds', *Cahiers Elisabethains*, 38, pp.25–40.

Greene, G 1980, '"The Power of Speech / to Stir Men's Blood": The Language of Tragedy in Shakespeare's *Julius Caesar*', *Renaissance Drama*, 11, pp. 67–93.

Hamer, M 1998, *William Shakespeare, Julius Caesar*, Writers and Their Work, Northcote House, Plymouth.

Hatchuel, S & Vienne-Guerrin, N (eds) 2009, *Shakespeare on Screen: The Roman Plays*, Publications des Universités de Rouen et du Havre, Rouen.

Howatson, MC (ed.) 1997, *The Oxford Companion to Classical Literature*, 2nd edition, Oxford University Press, Oxford.

Jehne, M 2005, 'History's Alternative Caesars: *Julius Caesar* and the Current Historiography', in H Zander, ed., *Julius Caesar: New Critical Essays*, Routledge, New York & London, pp.59–70.

Kahn, C 1997, *Roman Shakespeare: Warriors, Wounds, and Women*, Routledge, New York & London.

Liebler, NC 1998, 'What Portia knew', *Shakespeare*, vol 2, no.3, pp.17–19.

Loughrey, B 1992, '"I am no orator"; the language of public spaces', in L Cookson & B Loughrey, eds, *Julius Caesar*, Longman Critical Essays, Longman, Harlow, New York, pp.66–78.

McClelland, J 1987, 'Text, rhetoric, meaning', *Text*, vol 3, pp.11–26.

McMurtry, J 1998, *Julius Caesar: A Guide to the Play*, Greenwood Press, London.

Miles, G 1996, *Shakespeare and the Constant Romans*, Clarendon Press Oxford.

Miola, R 1987, 'Shakespeare and His Sources: Observations on the Critical History of *Julius Caesar*', *Shakespeare Survey*, vol 40, pp.69–76.

Munro, I 2005, *The Figure of the Crowd in Early Modern London: The City and its Double*, Palgrave Macmillan, New York & Hampshire.

Parker, B 2005, 'From Monarchy to Tyranny: Julius Caesar among Shakespeare's Roman Works', in H Zander, ed., *Julius Caesar: New Critical Essays*, Routledge, New York & London, pp.111–26.

Paster, GK 1989, '"In the spirit of men there is no blood": Blood as trope of gender in *Julius Caesar*', *Shakespeare Quarterly*, vol 40, pp. 284–86.

Patterson, A 1989, *Shakespeare and the Popular Voice*, Basil Blackwell, Oxford.

Ronan, C 2005, 'Caesar on and Off the Renaissance English Stage' in H Zander, ed., *Julius Caesar: New Critical Essays*, Routledge, New York & London, pp.71–89.

Rothwell, K & Melzer, A 1990, *Shakespeare on Screen: An International Filmography and Vidoegraphy*, Neal Schuman Publishers, New York.

Thomas, V 1992, *Julius Caesar*, Harvester Wheatsheaf, New York.

——2005, 'Shakespeare's Sources: Translations, Transformations, and Intertextuality in H Zander, ed., *Julius Caesar: New Critical Essays*, Routledge, New York & London, pp.91–110.

Traversi, D 1963, *Shakespeare: The Roman Plays*, Hollis & Carter, London.

Velz, JW 1971, 'Undular Structure in *Julius Caesar*', *Modern Language Review*, vol. 66, pp.21–30.

Zander, H (ed.) 2005, *Julius Caesar: New Critical Essays*, Routledge, New York & London.

Films

Julius Caesar 1953, dir. Joseph L. Mankiewicz, MGM, US. Starring Marlon Brando, John Gielgud, James Mason and Louis Calhern.

Julius Caesar 1970, dir. Stuart Burge, Commonwealth United, UK. Starring Charlton Heston, Jason Robards and John Gielgud.

Julius Caesar 1978, dir. Herbert Wise, BBC. Starring Richard Pasco, Charles Gray and Keith Michell.

Julius Caesar – Shakespeare: the Animated Tales 1996, dir. Yuri Kulakov, BBC, UK and Russia.